FIRST

HOME,

FOREVER

HOME

To Ken:
One of the first DDR
supporters. Thank you
for believing in our
work all these
years. Gratefully,
Lou

Thank you Nicole Bruckman for creating the book cover artwork

Thank you Luisa Mani for the book layout and graphics

This book is dedicated to
our Shelter Intervention counselor,
Amanda Casarez

INTRO:

Ana* came into the South Los Angeles Shelter, carrying her Chihuahua mix, Tomás, wrapped in a blanket like a baby. She was there to surrender him, she told shelter workers. She placed the dog on the receiving area counter, but her eyes were so sad a staff member wondered if she had doubts about what she was doing.

"Would you be willing to talk to a counselor about other options?" he asked. She nodded, and he directed her to an adjoining office where a young woman sat behind a desk.

"I'm Amanda, and I work for Downtown Dog Rescue's Shelter Intervention Program," the young woman said. "Is there something I can do that would help you keep your dog?"

Ana burst into tears.. She opened the blanket covering her dog to reveal an open wound covering his side. Amanda gasped. It looked like someone had set the poor dog on fire.

"He's dying," Ana wept.

She had been walking Tomás near her home when suddenly a big stray dog attacked, snarling and tearing at the little Chihuahua. Ana kicked at the other dog, desperately pulling Tomás's leash until she got him away, then took him straight to a local emergency vet. Cleaning and stabilizing the wound cost $4,000, which

Ana paid with her credit card, though it meant she would be completely maxed out. She was in her 50s and divorced, her son grown; Tomás was her only companion. The emergency room staff told Ana she'd need to take Tomás to his regular vet for follow-up care, and warned her that $4,000 was probably only the beginning of what treatment would cost – the final tab might be double that. Ana made $9.00 an hour. Just to pay off the credit card balance she'd deplete her life savings and have to borrow from family. Raising thousands more was literally impossible.

For the next few weeks, she did the best she could on her own using the painkillers and antibiotics the emergency vet gave her. She made sure to keep Tomás's bandage clean. But the wound got infected and started to fester, and she could tell that her beloved dog was in terrible pain. She felt heartbroken, helpless. She'd tried so hard to be a good pet owner – she'd had Tomás neutered as a puppy, kept his vaccinations current, never took him out without his collar, tags and leash. But without money, there was nothing she could do for him. If she surrendered her dog to the shelter, surely someone there would see what a good boy he was, take pity, and save his life.

Amanda called me. I'm the founder of Downtown Dog Rescue (DDR) and in April, 2013, I began our Shelter Intervention Program because I believe that the most effective way to reduce our nation's shelter population is not to take pets *out* of the shelter, but to prevent them from entering in the first place. When members of the South Los Angeles community are unable to reclaim impounded pets from the city shelter, or when they come in actively intending to surrender a dog or cat, we help them find a way to take their animals home instead.

"Can we help her?" Amanda asked.

I didn't even have to think about it. This pet owner didn't "want" to turn in her dog; she loved him deeply. She simply didn't have the money to pay for the care he needed.

I told Amanda that we would hold a fundraiser for Ana and Tomás. Amanda then called Teri Austin, a long-time DDR's partner and supporter, and president and medical director of the Amanda Foundation, which runs Dr. Shipps Animal Hospital in Beverly Hills. Teri arranged for Tomás to be treated. It cost $1,500 for surgery to re-open, cleanse and close his wound, and six weeks of recuperation and antibiotic therapy. The little dog survived, and within 48 hours, our wonderful supporters raised the money we needed to pay for his care.

Ana could barely believe it. "Thank you so much," she said, crying again. "Without you, I would have lost my best friend. It would have broken my heart."

That Tomás's story had a happy ending was a small miracle. But it was not an *unusual* miracle. In the slightly more than two years our intervention program has operated, we've kept over 5,000 pets from entering this high-intake, low-adoption shelter located in one of the city's most densely populated, low-income and underserved neighborhoods. Working to change both the lives of animals *and* the people who care for them, we've provided free or reduced price spay and neuter services, funded vaccinations, and paid for medical care ranging from treatment of manage to orthopedic surgery for broken bones. We've covered humane euthanasia for pets that were terminally ill and suffering. We've made hundreds of home improvements, like putting up secure fences and installing dog runs when a lack of those things made it impossible for people to retain their pets. And when despite all our efforts we realized that pets needed to be re-homed, we took care of that, too.

We've received numerous grants and awards for our work. More important to us, we've been recognized as a good neighbor and resource by the people we serve. We've also been thrilled to see our work spread. In November, 2013, Kerry Lowe, a volunteer at the city's North Central Shelter, started the nonprofit Home Dog LA, and began an intervention program modeled on ours. In February, 2015, we partnered with the group Rescue Train to open a second program, at the East Valley Animal Shelter.

Intervention is a new and exciting way to improve animal welfare in an at-risk community, and an important part of advancing a national dialogue. We in animal rescue have talked a lot about the 3-4 million cats and dogs that still die in America's shelters each year. All of us have worked tirelessly, and still do, to change those numbers. We pull animals, treat them, transport them thousands of miles, do everything in our power to find

8

them new homes. But we have only so many hours to save shelter animals, only so many pet lovers to take them in.

Some of us are beginning to ask: Why are we not doing more to make pets' first homes their forever homes? Why haven't we worked to stop the "voluntary" surrender of pets that sustains the flood of animals into public shelters? I'm asking that we take those questions even further: Why aren't we doing more to help the people who care for those animals? Why aren't we giving them more pet care information? Why aren't we providing affordable vaccinations, emergency medical services, spay/neuter, pet food, training – the support that will allow families on the edge to retain and properly care for their animals?

These are urgent, important questions. More, working to answer them makes practical sense. On average, owner surrender accounts for *30 percent* of the animals entering our country's public shelters. Notice that wording: *on average*. The numbers are far higher in poor neighborhoods. There are many reasons why, and we'll get to them. But in general, we in the rescue movement have not focused our energy on helping pet owners in those communities. Instead, we've demonized those who surrender their animals, calling them "uncaring," and "irresponsible," without taking the time to understand the very real challenges they face. When I walk through a shelter and see the dogs and cats in their cages, I know that many of them were loved, and that the person who loved them saw no alternative to surrender because he or she faced eviction, homelessness, overcrowding, destitution. Programs and services that might have helped were too difficult to access or required proof of need to qualify. Even reclaiming a lost pet from the shelter can be difficult, since it requires identification that matches the address where the pet owner lives – a challenge for people in transition. It's daunting to navigate a system that you don't understand because you're uneducated, don't speak English, or are unable to read in any language.

Awareness that we must find new ways to deal with this issue is growing. I get calls daily, from small rescues to national organizations, all wanting to understand our model so they can adapt it for use. Whenever I speak, I'm swarmed by people who want to start an intervention in their own city or town. If you're reading this, you've probably had similar thoughts. I believe that intervention is the future of animal sheltering. **The average cost to keep an animal out of the shelter is only $50.00. Imagine if the tax dollars we now spend on housing, feeding – and euthanizing – shelter populations went instead to providing low-income communities with the resources they need to care for their animals at home.**

This book is a manual to help the many people who've asked for guidance in setting up intervention programs. We'll walk you through the why of intervention as well as the practical aspects of setting up a program, talk about the challenges we've faced, the best practices we've developed, what's succeeded (and hasn't). We want our effort to spread. We can talk all we want about "No Kill," a phrase, a goal, an ideal that doesn't even mean the same thing to all those who use it. But if we're serious about improving conditions for pets, we must help people, and if we mean to make lasting improvements in animal sheltering, we must factor poor people's pets into the equation. We must stop judging and setting up artificial barriers of "us" and "them." We're on the same side. Our love for animals connects us – and caring for these animals connects us to each other.

I come back again and again to one basic truth: **The enormous number of pets still coming into our shelter system, many of which will die there, is not a pet problem. It is not a people problem. It is a poverty problem.**

This understanding is at the root of everything we do.

Chapter 1: Working With What Is

Before I say anything else, it's important to explain the community in which DDR's intervention program operates, as well as how we got here. The lessons we learned along the way have been key to our program's success.

The South L.A. Shelter is high-intake because the community around it is stressed. Side by side, both people and animals suffer. The densely-packed 50-square-mile neighborhood of South Los Angeles has a population of around 750,000 and the highest overall poverty rate in Los Angeles County. Around 40 percent of the people who live here are struggling just to make ends meet, and if you include undocumented immigrants, the "shadow population," the numbers would be far higher. (South LA is about 40 percent African-American and 57 percent Latino.) I'm not talking about "I can't afford to go to the movies" struggling, I mean the desperation of "I can't feed my kids." Around 370,000 people (that we know of) are unemployed. More men and women are under-employed, work part time when they would prefer to work full time, work a low-wage job – or two or three – or operate in the informal economy, for instance recycling bottles and paper. The high school drop-out rate is 50 percent. Sixty-five percent of the people who live here are renters, in a city that has the biggest gap in the nation between rent price and average wage. We also have the city's second highest rate of homelessness.

Poverty affects every aspect of life. According to a 2009 National Institutes of Health Study, just living in a socio-economically deprived area can lead to weight gain and a greater risk of dying at an early age. In our neighborhood, where 73 percent of restaurants are fast-food outlets and we have less than an acre of public parkland per 1,000 people, 33 percent of area children are overweight, and one in seven residents has diabetes. One city analysis found that on average a man or woman living in Brentwood (an affluent West LA neighborhood) lived 12 years longer than a resident of South LA's Watts.

South LA is a hard place to be a child. Studies of South and East LA kids have found that 90 percent of them had witnessed or experienced violence and violent crime. As a result, some suffer PTSD, others depression. We know from other research that those who suffer "adverse childhood experiences" like violence and severe family dysfunction and don't get help to deal with it are at increased risk for problems that range from academic failure to substance abuse. (Or worse: since the 1990s, the suicide rate among black children has doubled.) Exhausted, desperate, reeling from crisis to crisis, poor men, women and children sometimes make bad decisions that exacerbate their situations.

Because South LA is a tough place for people, it is hard for animals, too. We don't even have a way to count the area's dog and cat populations. Some are licensed,

13

but more are informally adopted or "community" animals – fed by many, but belonging to no one – or roam the streets as strays. Ten thousand a year pass through the shelter. The combination of poverty, lack of education and neighborhood deprivation makes it hard to be a responsible owner. Veterinarians are few and far between, and without affordable vaccinations, we see outbreaks of parvo and distemper, disease that are virtually unheard of in more affluent parts of the city. Increased access to affordable, convenient spay and neuter services is just beginning to make a major impact in the number of unplanned litters.

The challenge of improving conditions for both people and pets in this community are enormous, and doing so respectfully and productively is especially difficult for anyone who grew up with a different frame of reference. As Father Gregory Boyle, a hero in the gang prevention and intervention movement, put it, "What we need is a compassion that stands in awe at the burdens the poor have to carry, rather than stands in judgment at the way they carry it."

I was fortunate that my work in the years before I came to South LA taught me that lesson.

The founding of Downtown Dog Rescue in 1996 grew from my shock at the animals I saw in the streets of downtown Los Angeles and my desire to give them something better.

I ended up downtown by chance. After some struggles in my 20s, at 31 I went back to school, hoping to become a teacher. I have a good eye and I've always been interested in design, so I paid my bills by buying furniture in thrift stores, restoring the pieces, and selling them at upscale flea markets. At one, I met Frank Novak, co-founder of the downtown LA-based furniture manufacturing company, Modernica. Frank took a chance, and hired me as his assistant.

The job sent me into another world. I grew up in a working-class Southern California city, with parents who raised me to be afraid of "bums" and "winos." Suddenly I was going to work at a factory near Skid Row, during the years when a crack epidemic was destroying the community. The desperation and chaos was almost beyond description. Every day, I saw people living in tents in alleys and homeless settlements big enough to look like a refugee camp in the developing world. The sidewalks were covered with trash, bottles, crack pipes, rats, human waste. Mental illness and addiction were everywhere -- people walked down the street half-naked, talking to themselves, screaming, fighting.

The people scared me, but the dogs broke my heart. I saw them tied to fences to serve as guard dogs, or running through alleys scrounging for food, emaciated, wounded, lying in piles of garbage nursing litters of puppies. Or dead: The factory was close to the LA Produce Mart, and the gutters always held the body of some street dog that had been hit by a truck.

No one in the neighborhood seemed to notice, or they just considered this misery normal. For me, it was unacceptable. When I was a kid, my family's German

Shepherd, Heidi (who we bought from a breeder, back in the days when we didn't know better), was my rock. Whenever anything went wrong in my life, I held her, and things felt less frightening. My childhood dream was to be a vet. Within a few months after I arrived on Skid Row, I teamed up with a co-worker Richard Tuttlemondo, to drive around trying to trap street dogs and take them to be spayed.

I soon learned that many of downtown dogs weren't strays, but had owners: homeless men and women. I offered them help with their dogs -- bags of food, flea medicine -- and came to know them as individuals rather than the "bums" of my childhood. We had something in common: love for animals. Some of them had rescued their dogs from storm drains and dumpsters, and saved their lives.

With time, I became an advocate for these men and women, and a liaison with Los Angeles Animal Services. On the streets, I got the nickname Dog Rescue Lady, and even animal control officers started calling me when a homeless dog owner had lost his pet or had it confiscated because he'd been arrested, then couldn't afford to redeem it. Sometimes I used my own money to recover those animals and return them to their owners. The street was a hard life, but I knew these animals would never be adopted or make the transition into life in a suburban home.

My friend and intervention program partner Larry Hill was a clerk at the North Central Animal Shelter during those days. In 2002, he watched, mystified, as I redeemed the same dog over and over for a homeless veteran with a drug problem who was caught in an endless cycle of brief incarcerations, during which his dog would be impounded, and after which he couldn't afford to bail him out.

One day he asked, "Why are you helping this guy?"

"Because he loves his dog and takes good care of it," I said.

Larry immediately understood. He knew that this dog was doomed in the shelter, and the absurd rules that kept it there by making redemption so expensive: Redemption fees were higher if the dog wasn't licensed, but it was impossible to get a license if you were homeless, since animal services demanded an address. I'd offered to let the homeless veteran use my office address but animal services said no, because he didn't "really" live there.

Larry quietly accepted my address and entered it into the system. Dog license granted, problem solved. Over the next few years, he did the same for around 300 more Skid Row dogs, all of which were microchipped with my work phone number, so if they ended up at the shelter, I could get them out. I will always owe Larry an enormous debt.

Over the years, I brought mobile spay/neuter clinics into downtown, took the dogs of homeless men and women to the veterinary hospital when necessary, listened to people's stories of how they ended up on the street, and learned how to talk to the confused and mentally ill. Sometimes I was told that "You're the first person I've talked to who isn't paid for it." And I spent enough time on the sidewalks and in the encampments to learn that you can't be effective with struggling people unless you treat them with the same courtesy and respect that you'd want yourself.

Sometimes I took in dogs that had no homes or had lost their people, an effort that evolved into a more traditional rescue. For a long time I housed those dogs for adoption at my home and in a kennel at the rear of the Modernica factory. Downtown Dog Rescue operated on Skid Row until 2005, when we moved out and into the community of South Los Angeles and City of Compton. DDR has been covered by major media, received grants from national organizations, and in 2013, when the Modernica land was sold and the factory relocated, we raised over $350,000, including a $100,000 gift from Best Friends Animal Society, to purchase land and build a beautiful kennel in nearby South Gate. It's now home to 25 adoptable dogs (and a few permanent residents). The full DDR story spans almost 20 years, and will have to be told another time.

But by the time we started the intervention program, I knew that if you approached a community with honesty, humility, and a willingness to learn, that you could win their trust – and accomplish almost anything.

***

Working With What Is: Key Points

- Thirty percent of the nation's shelter animals are owner surrenders

- Owner surrender is highest in poor areas, because poverty challenges people's ability to care for their pets

- If animal activists work actively *with* the poor we can changes these outcomes, improving the lives of both people and pets

***

Chapter 2: Getting Started

If you're reading this, perhaps you imagine I'm going to offer you a blueprint for beginning a successful shelter intervention project. But here's the secret: To start a program...start a program.

I'm not trying to be cute – taking a first step really is key. If you overthink what you're trying to do, believe you have to do everything at once, or spend your time debating endless "what if"s, you'll just paralyze yourself. I often have people come up to me at conferences, crying and telling me that "Maybe I can do something like this...someday... when the kids are grown... when I retire...when I have the money to buy a truck and ten acres of land..."

I answer, as kindly as I can, "Why are you making everything so difficult?"

It took more than a decade of rescue work before I completely understood the need for intervention, and in retrospect, I was lucky that when I began I had no idea what I was doing. That let me start small, feel free to experiment, and keep my expectations minimal.

This work isn't simple. Underserved communities with pet relinquishment problems aren't places you can "fix," and you can't even help if you're trying to follow a rigid formula and set of rules. Anyone who wants to use our model will have to adapt the program and specifics to match his or her community and adjust still more later, depending on what succeeds or doesn't.

Based on our experiences, however, I can suggest guidelines to help you focus as you begin.

To repeat: The point of a shelter intervention program is to keep pets out of the shelter by helping them stay in the homes they already have. *How* that's done varies by community because the factors that cause people to surrender or lose their pets are different in different places. That means your first work is doing some research.

Where do you want to work?

The fast answer to that question is "a community with economic challenges, where I think I can do some good." In the best case scenario, you know where you want to work through personal experience. You're a volunteer at a shelter where there's a high kill rate and see the same reason for relinquishment again and again. Or you work as part of a rescue group that keeps taking animals from the same area. Or you live in a community where there's an ongoing problem of lost dogs, stray dogs, community cats no one cares for, or dog bites occurring too frequently. You know of or live in an area that is underserved on many levels, not just for pets. Maybe you volunteer at a school, where you hear stories. You know of an area with no animal hospitals, or there's only one, and it's super expensive. You care about this community and believe that "If only we had _____, things would be better."

It's also possible to locate the kind of area where intervention could help. Look for economic disenfranchisement, since poverty and relinquishment rates go together. School ratings are another clue – typically the lower the rating, the greater the need for pet assistance. The higher the crime rate – especially the rate of violent crime – and the greater the number of registered sex offenders in the area, the greater the need for help of all kinds.

If you're part of the community where you want to work, you'll have the connections and relationships to move the program along quickly. If not, you'll have to build them, which starts with getting to know your target area deeply, intimately and on every level. This knowledge goes far beyond anything you can learn on Google – you've got to spend time and talk to people. When we began in South LA, one of the first things I did was to volunteer at the Watts public library. When you work in the library, you meet people and they talk to you about their lives. They remember: *She gave my daughter a book*. Now you're known, an advocate and friend. If you ask friends and colleagues, you may find that one of them grew up in your target neighborhood, or has a relative living there, someone who can sit down with you and teach you about it. Your role then is to listen and learn.

You also could hire an advisory team of a few locals, and pay them to do the work of finding out the community's biggest struggles and needs. High shelter intake areas usually also have high unemployment, and some of those who'd like to volunteer can't afford to work for free. The offer to pay for labor is respectful and solves that problem.

How well do you know the people you hope to serve? Remember that the focus of our intervention program is helping pets *and* people. You can't work with the people of your community unless you can communicate. What language(s) do they speak? What's their heritage? If your area is largely immigrant, where are people's home countries, and what were common practices and cultural expectations there? The more you know about people who aren't like you, the less likely it is you will see them through cultural bias, or worse, as "those people." Just because someone is needy doesn't mean he or she doesn't want to or deserve to be treated with respect. Just because a program offers a free service does not mean those who receive it should be asked to accept poor quality, not ask questions or "line up and shut up." When I worked downtown, one of my best teachers was Benny Josephs. Benny was an African American from New Orleans, a former security guard who lost his job after he was shot, and was now disabled and a functioning alcoholic. He lived in an alley, in a cardboard refrigerator box he shared with his dog, Ironhead. (And, until I got to work, a changing group of unspayed female dogs and ongoing litters of puppies.) He was a master storyteller, and one of the sweetest people I've ever known. He also had a good sense of what was real. Back then, church groups regularly came down to

Skid Row to "feed the homeless." Benny saw right through them.

"They don't care about us," he said. "They come with food, but they don't talk to no one, they wear rubber gloves and they get out as fast as they can. They're just trying to score points to get to heaven."

What are the biggest challenges that people and pets in your target community face?
Different communities have different needs. In some places, the biggest challenge may be a breed ban, in others – for instance, many metropolitan areas, where it can cost thousands to rent a small house or apartment -- lack of affordable housing will be the big thing. What would best help address that challenge? Can you offer it? *You need to be sure that what you want to provide is what people really need.* If it isn't, you might waste your time, or worse, offend the people you want to help. We all know that getting an animal microchipped is a great way to make sure a lost pet gets home. So can you keep animals out of the shelter by offering to subsidize microchipping? Not if the dogs and cats are being surrendered by their owners, or if owners don't have the money to pay for fencing adequate to keep their animals in, or to reclaim them from the shelter when they're found.

As you look at your target community's challenges, consider which ones truly arouse your passion.

24

You want to work on something you care strongly about, not what a foundation is offering a grant for this month or what meets some arbitrary definition of "important." Not something that everyone else is doing, because you think that will make it easier to get donations. The work you tackle should be something that fascinates you, bothers you, keeps you up at night. Something your friends complain you talk about all the time. Something that makes you feel strong emotion – anger, curiosity, righteous rage – but not so upset and sad that you won't be able to work effectively.

Take your time. This isn't something you can figure out in a weekend. (And because getting to know a community deeply and working on its problem does take a lot of time, when you choose your location, pick somewhere that's relatively convenient to where you live.) In my early years on Skid Row, I volunteered at a lot of established rescues, and at first I thought there was something wrong with me because I didn't feel as passionately engaged during those hours as I did when I was downtown. That's how I knew my work on the street was my true calling. When you follow what engages you, it almost always leads you to higher and higher levels of involvement. On Skid Row, I went after the dogs, which led me to the people. Staying true to your own mission helps you make significant change in the world around you.

What realities of your chosen community will impact your ability to work there?

25

When I first started working in South Los Angeles, I set up a spay/neuter clinic, in what I thought was a relatively central location. I got plenty of pet owners to come, but only residents from one side of town. I couldn't figure out why. Then an active gang member (a very nice person, who supported my effort) explained that my clinic was in one gang's turf. Anyone associated with a rival group was never going to come. To enable your effort to succeed, and to keep you and your volunteers safe, you've got to find out what the street rules are. Are there gangs? Areas where it's actively unsafe to go? Informal boundaries that residents will not cross? If that's so, what must you do to work around the problem?

Once you have a goal, set an interim goal to reach first

When you do important work, your first step is always a small one. Think realistically about what you hope to achieve, and what tools and funds you currently have to help you. Then set an intermediate goal that's simple, and (more important) attainable. In my early days on Skid Row, that was trying to catch and spay a few street dogs. Another interim step was reaching out to homeless dog owners with a bag of food for the dogs and a sandwich for them. If your eventual hope is to set up an intervention program in an underserved community, an early goal might be to distribute some dog food once a week at a neighborhood park. It could be to address a local church group about spay and neuter. Only offer to do what you really can do, and only do what you can do well. I promise that once you take that first step, the way forward will become clear. You'll build on your early results and get to the next level. Or you'll fail, which is also okay. If that's what happens, pause, regroup and learn more before you try again.

Make good friends and keep them close

As you work within your target community, stay true to yourself and you'll find the allies you need. Good people are attracted to those who have a purpose and goals. Many of the people who are now part of the intervention program are men and women I've known for years. Larry Hill, the former North Central Shelter staff member who bent the rules to help me register dogs is a dog trainer. He runs a class for us and comes to all our events, not only as a trainer, but as a senior member of the local community, someone with prestige and credibility. Teri Austin of the Amanda Foundation, who helped with Downtown Dog Rescue's spay and neuter program, has partnered on a number of family-friendly clinics that were also community-wide celebrations in South LA, Watts, and Compton.

Cornelius Austin, aka Dogman, was someone I started working with over ten years ago, after a homeless man I knew died and left me his dog Petey. Petey had already bitten five people, and nobody else would help me try to train him. Dogman grew up in South LA., once bred pit bulls, then began a Sunday training class, free, for anyone who had problems with a dog. Dogman got me to a point where I could put Petey in a down-stay 20 feet out and have him recall, and for both of us, that was huge. Petey stayed with me -- he died this year, just short of his 18th birthday -- and Dogman and I are still friends. He has his own following and fan page, his free Sunday class. These days it's almost all rescues.

I also rely on people I've met in the course of working in the community – the leaders, loudmouths, the neighbors with opinions, the church women not shy to tell me what I'm doing wrong. When I first moved my work from downtown to South LA, I wanted to host a mobile spay and neuter clinic. I went to the Tower of Faith Church, which kindly let us use their parking lot for the event; Rosalie, a community member who lived down the street from the church, helped spread the word, then became one of our regular volunteers. We've hosted free monthly mobile clinics ever since. I even reached out to the police, and we've held clinics at a local police station. Loving animals is something we can all come together over.

As Steve Harvey put it in one of my favorite books, *Act Like a Success, Think Like a Success,* "God has already lined up all the people in your path to get you to your dreams and your visions."

Put together an intervention team

If you're aiming to have a mostly-volunteer intervention program, it requires a small, but super solid group of people who know and trust each other. Your program's early days will be challenging and a time of

28

great vulnerability. You need to feel free to send each other nasty emails saying "I hate everything and this was a mistake," or to be able to cry with someone who'll hear you but remind you of the bigger picture. Even after things get off the ground, the work can take over your life. Team members need to set boundaries for each other, and for everyone volunteering with the program.

The ideal intervention team has these elements:

A pack leader. The program can't be run by committee or consensus vote. Things happen fast when someone's at the shelter to surrender a pet, and decisions on how to respond have to be made equally quickly. Someone has to make them, and take responsibility for them. I am the one, for instance, who makes the on-the-spot decision about spending a large sum of money for a difficult intervention case. Our counselor Amanda will phone or text me, and though I'm at my other (paying) job, I will make the time to answer.

Someone has to fix things when they go wrong, or shoulder the blame when they can't be fixed. A pack leader actually may not get to work too much with the animals; she's the one who gets to clean up messes and step in when everyone else is on Christmas vacation. As with any business, the leader has to have the vision and enthusiasm to keep everyone's energy up and the outlook positive.

An intervention team also needs **someone practical**, because the need you'll face is bottomless, and the ability to say "no" is important. I'm terrible at this -- if I'm at the shelter and see two girls crying over the dog

29

they're giving up because it's sick and their grandma has to go back to Mexico, I'll want to do whatever it takes or costs to send that dog home with them. I have a steering committee of seven that I can count on to tell me, "I know you want to do this, but we can't afford it."

Ideally, you should have **a math nerd** -- maybe a volunteer who's better with numbers than at interacting with people. We live in an age when funders will ask you to prove anything you say you've learned or done. It's vital to record data: how many pets you've saved, how many people you've assisted, what ethnicity and economic level they are, what zip codes they live in, how many are male, female, single mothers... Even when you're just beginning and there seems no point to it, record the data. Eventually, those numbers will help you tailor and get grants.

A PR-savvy person is valuable, someone with connections, who's good at talking to donors and dog food companies -- the friend you have who's never at the shelter without bringing a camera or a reporter. She or he can distill your message into a pitch, which will help you fundraise.

You need a **number of worker bees.** These volunteers have lives full of other obligations – demanding jobs, kids in school – and can only give you scattered pieces of time. But they can fill in, check records, transport dogs. Don't burn them out by asking them to do too much and always thank them for whatever they can do.

You also need **volunteers with practical skills** like carpentry and home repair. The families that we help commonly blame their animal problems on "the new neighbors' dog" or "the landlord" when the problem is actually too many pets in too little space. Families routinely live on lots with two or three houses, or with others in a single-family home that's been subdivided. Dogs not well separated often "fence fight" and make trouble, or end up chained and tethered, which is illegal, and can lead to citations. Our skilled volunteers put up metal sheets along fences so animals can't get at each other, and repair gates to keep them in and secure.

Most important of all, you need a dedicated and empathetic **counselor** who will be the one to interact with the people and families who come to the shelter in crisis. This is the one job that we've made a paying position – it's that demanding and that crucial. A shelter intervention counselor has to be flexible, patient, skilled enough to deal with animals that are sick, injured, aggressive or shy, and people who are grief-stricken, furious, arrogant, surly, withdrawn, unpredictable, and even mentally ill. She can face anything in a single day, and often does.

When the shelter intervention program first began, I thought I needed to hire a counselor with an MBA or experience in management. Then I met our counselor, Amanda Arreola, when she volunteered at a couple of DDR clinics, and knew she was the one. Amanda lived in South LA, and knew its people because she's just like them. Her background was working to empower local youth; she also loved animals and was in the process of starting her own rescue. When we talked, I saw that she had the same passionate desire that I do to help people with pets. She's been with us for two years, and I can't imagine the program without her. Amanda, who speaks Spanish and understands the circumstances of the undocumented, gives us access to South LA's shadow population. She's a great salesperson, the one who must persuade someone who has already made up his or her mind to surrender an animal to *change* it. She sells the program. In some ways, animal welfare is no different than any other business. Modernica, where I make my living, would go bankrupt fast if it wasn't good at convincing people to buy its products.

If you're in a community that's not English-speaking, you must have a bilingual counselor. If you're in a community not your own, the best of all worlds is being able to pay someone who is local to be your counselor. You're creating a job, recycling dollars within the area. Whenever I see amazing volunteers, I ask what they do for a living, I tell them my vision, and that I'm not able to pay people to work for me right now, but one day, I will be.

When we began our second intervention effort at the East Valley Shelter, we began slowly, with one day of paid and two days of volunteer labor per week. We found our paid counselor through an ad on Craigslist. The woman I hired had never been to an animal shelter or even owned a pet. But she was a graduate student training to be a social worker, which meant she understood the human element of what we try to do. That was what was important; she could learn about ear infections and mange.

I think it's counterproductive to get too focused on finding the "perfect hire." What works today may not be what you need a year from now. The key is finding someone willing to learn, and who wants to grow and adapt.

A final point: A good counselor is also creative, a problem-solver, thoughtful, and aware that what we do has limits: **A shelter intervention program aims for a compassionate outcome for people and animals in crisis. It does not – cannot – "fix" people's lives. My years on Skid Row taught me that you must meet people where they are, and let go of the rest.**

Make strategic alliances
--With Animal Control

It goes without saying that a good intervention program – especially one like ours, which is based at the shelter itself – needs the support, or at least permission, of the local animal services department and shelter staff. We are very appreciative of Los Angeles Animal Services, which trusted us to run this program, and for all the support we receive from LAAS staff and volunteers. Make an appointment with whoever runs animal services in your community, as well as the head of the shelter where you want to work, and be professional enough to understand that this is a bureaucracy where everything is planned ahead of time. You're not going to roll in all excited and get welcomed with open arms and told to start next week. You also need to know whether or not the shelter is union, because often there are rules that nothing can be done if it takes away a union job. Write down exactly what you are proposing to do, what your work will mean to the shelter, what staff will get out of it, and why your work will not negatively affect them:

"We're going to get a grant to offer free spay and neuter services for these five zip codes in your area, and once a month we'd like to set up a card table in front of the receiving area with posters and fliers offering information about this service. Increased sterilization rates will help reduce shelter intake, both of intact animals and unplanned litters. We won't be in your way, and what we do won't impact the shelter staff's regular schedules or responsibilities."

You might also point out what past work or connections give you credibility: "We've run food banks...we've done pet transport...we have contact with a dog trainer willing to give some hours... I'm a photographer, and I'm happy to come into the shelter and take pictures of available animals for your website."

In general, shelter staffs work hard and get blamed for a lot of things that aren't their fault. Imagine you have to have to face killing animals every day as part of your job responsibility, then get attacked as the reason they're dying, because you're not adopting out enough. If they say no to your plan, listen. They may have been burned in the past, they may need to get to know you better, they may want to see you in partnership with a large national

34

organization. "No" doesn't mean responding with "I hate this person, I spent hours on this plan and she ripped it to shreds. Let's go on Facebook and get her fired!" It means, "I learned a lot writing this – including that I shouldn't have spent so much time on it. Next time, I'll write a paragraph and get feedback and talk to animal control before I do the rest."

--With veterinarians

Finding local veterinarians who'll work with you and give your families a break is essential. We work with several, and it took time to build the network. Geography and price were our top considerations. We started with a list of hospitals close to the South LA Shelter where we work, then created a spreadsheet of services that we wanted to offer, and asked every volunteer in our program if they had any contacts. If they did, we handed them the sheet, which listed the prices we could pay and asked the volunteer to set up meetings with vets and/or their office managers. We gave them a script that helped them explain how the program worked – we wanted everyone to explain it the same way – then put all the information into a Google Doc. One volunteer was in charge of collecting and entering the replies: where the various doctors and hospitals were located, what services they would commit to at what prices, whether or not an appointment was necessary, and what days and hours they were available. With that information, we created a master spreadsheet for our counselor, and maps to each facility, so no one we sent to for medical care would get lost. In practice, we hand pet owners a voucher detailing what services we are going to cover, at what price, and a map of how to get to the hospital. To clarify: We pay the service provider; we don't hand out cash. Often our counselor will call ahead to give the vet's office our pet owner's information, and to double-check that he or she can be seen that day.

Many of the people we help rely on public transportation or have to make arrangement to borrow a car. We never want to send someone on a trip only to find out the vet is out sick or is closing early that day. We're also grateful that thanks to the Sam Simon Foundation we can provide a mobile clinic to perform surgeries for low income families free of charge.

How did we convince private vets to work affordably? We had to build trust. Remember: veterinarians are in business; they have to make a living. I wanted anyone willing to work with me to be confident that he or she would get paid. And so there were times I went to their offices to say, "You don't know me, and I'm going to be sending you patients who don't have good credit. I'm going to write you a check right now for $1,000, which you can consider a security deposit." When you do something like that, people take you seriously.

We also knew no one person could offer everything, so we asked if there were certain services each particular vet could or would do at a reduced rate. Many agreed according to their priorities. One vet we know became especially upset when I explained that one of the reasons poor people sometimes relinquish a very

36

old or sick pet is because it's in terrible pain and they don't know what else to do – they've never heard of humane euthanasia. He said that he would do the procedure for us at his cost, so all our cases of humane euthanasia go to him. We use another vet for vaccinations, another for surgery, etc. If vets are inspired to offer a service at an amazing price, be careful not to burn them out!

By the way, I've used this same strategy with other providers we need, like trainers and groomers. And we tell everyone that whenever possible, we'll send also them paying customers. Or that if we get any media coverage, we'll be sure to mention them.

--With local rescues and animal welfare foundations

A sizable amount of the work we do is funded by foundations and large organizations. Funding from the ASPCA, for instance, enables us to perform 500 free spay/neuter surgeries per year. The Amanda Foundation hospital gives us great prices and services, and we would not have gotten off the ground without major financial assistance from Found Animals Foundation, which supports innovative work to reduce shelter euthanasia.

We also rely on small local rescues. While our program always strives to keep animals with their first families, realistically, that isn't always possible. When relinquishment becomes the only option, you can't keep an animal out of the shelter unless you have another place for it to go. That's where local rescues come in.

The more rescues willing to work with you the better, but quality is more important than quantity. Approach people you know are like-minded, and don't hesitate to ask for help with other things you do. Rescue group volunteers can help out at spay and neuter clinics, for instance, and you can offer them something in return: if you run this clinic with me, take all the pictures you want, use them to get donations to run your own clinic, and I'll help you. We work with a variety of local groups, including Noah's Bark, Ghetto Rescue Foundation, the Watts Project, Dawg Squad, Angel City Pit Bulls, Go Dog LA, A Purposeful Rescue, Bullies and Buddies, Love Leo Rescue, Wags and Walks, Kitt Crusaders, Kitty Bungalow, Stray Cat Alliance, and the Compassion Project.

--With providers of other supportive services your families may need
When you run an intervention program in an economically challenged community you confront a lot of problems that have nothing to do with pets. Find out where your pet owners can get every support service they might need: the local food bank, legal assistance and tenants' rights office, a trustworthy mechanic who doesn't charge a fortune, and a sliding scale therapist.

Think about money
Creating a shelter intervention program budget is a Catch-22 situation: You can't decide what to include

until you know what funds you have available, but often you can't raise money for a program until you show what it can do.

I self-funded a lot of the work I did at first, spending about $2,000 a year of my own money, which included $1,000 for the first community-wide spay and neuter clinic we sponsored. The clinic was subsidized by a grant from Petsmart, but that subsidy only covered residents who lived in the City of Los Angeles and owned a pitbull. The money I contributed allowed us to serve people who showed up but weren't covered by the grant. I spent the money because I wanted data, and I didn't want to wait. I knew I'd be applying for more grants, and I needed to prove that low-income people would spay and neuter their pets if it was free, and they didn't have to show ID.

This is the reality: No funder will write you a check for thousands of dollars because you have a good idea. When you show you had an intention and a plan that you then executed and analyzed, it's a different story. I'm talking about writing a report, just like you did in school: This is my hypothesis, this is what supports it, this is what we did and what happened – what worked, what was a surprise – and this is the result of my research. Offered with a nice graphic, like a pie chart, it will get you grants.

My feeling is that if you don't believe in your game plan enough to put your own money on the line, why would you expect anyone else to? On the other hand, I know that not everyone has the ability to self-fund, and I absolutely don't mean to suggest that anyone do anything that puts her in personal debt or financial jeopardy. In the animal welfare movement it's sometimes a badge of honor to spend all of your money saving animals rather than making enough to put your own house in order. That's a bad long-term strategy. You can't take care of people or animals if you can't take care of yourself. If you're stressed and anxious about money, you won't make good decisions. So look close to home: Are you, the leader of the program, financially organized and debt-free? If you're already stressed about money, running this program will drive you crazy. Before you do anything else, pay off all your debt and follow the same steps you'll be suggesting to the people who'll ask for help. The same holds true for a group. If your organization has no savings and great difficulty paying what it owes, get your finances in order. Unless you and your team are financially sound, you won't accomplish anything.

Even without self-funding, it's possible to work around the need to fund-raise, at least at first. Having a good working knowledge of programs that already exist for both animals and people will keep you from wasting time and effort. There's no point in reinventing the wheel. Maybe your local shelter offers free rabies shots once a week, but hasn't been so good at getting the word out to the community. That can be your job.

In 1999, when I was working on Skid Row, I learned that the City of Los Angeles had a brand new mobile pet clinic that no one knew about. I met the vet in charge, who told me that "we're having a hard time filling appointments."

A free program that wasn't being used because no one knew about it? That made me furious! We arranged to park the mobile clinic right in front of my factory, an area that was a ghost town on weekends, and got California Pizza Kitchen to donate pizzas, so we could feed anyone who brought an animal to be sterilized. I asked a couple of homeless guys I knew to pass out flyers on the street. The next time the mobile clinic came to my factory's neighborhood, there were 100 people and animals waiting in a line that went around the block. The surgeon, Dr. Bob Goldman, came out in his gown and mask and couldn't believe it. "I've never seen anything like this in my life!" he told me. Over time, we worked with Dr. Goldman to spay and neuter hundreds of dogs and cats.

(The passing out flyers detail in this story also shows that knowing your neighborhood enables you to work productively in it. One of the questions you need to ask yourself is how residents get their information. Publicizing events and services online or via email is convenient, but useless if your community members don't have computer access. Putting up posters at a big mall will reach too many outsiders. You need to think very specifically and very locally: Do people get a neighborhood newspaper? Is there a regular place they go for yard sales or a swap meet? Where does someone without transportation shop? Is there a big crowd on Tuesday at the food bank? Can you put up a banner at the

41

park? You always want announcements of upcoming events and serves to be displayed in places where your audience will actually see them.)

Another way to work with very little upfront money is to find programs that are partially subsidized, but still not affordable for your community, and filling the gap. If pet sterilization is offered for "only" $15 or $20, can your group pay that fee for someone who can't?

Are there great existing programs for which some of your community members can't qualify? The South LA shelter offered free and low-cost spay/neuter vouchers before we came along, but to qualify you had to provide ID and proof that you needed financial help. Residents who lived and worked off the books couldn't do that. So in addition to informing qualified residents about the city's program, we financed the others – including people whose homes were officially in Los Angeles *County*, even though they lived right across the street from the city boundary. It made no sense to us that they try to access the service and be turned away.

There are other ways to go cash-free. Sometimes it's easier to get donations of goods than of money. Perhaps a local grocery store, pet store, Target or Wal-Mart might be willing to give you collars or leashes or surplus/expired pet food if you picked them up. You can hold a food pantry for animals one Saturday a month, a win-win situation: You're not spending money you don't have and would need to raise, and you're there in the community making your presence felt.

Another easy option: create an Amazon Wishlist and share it on Facebook. (I'll cover the need for a social media presence in the next chapter.) My latest Wish List was for 20 bags of dog food for a "Family Dog Day" that I wanted to hold at a local park. I posted the request at 5:00 AM when I was drinking my morning coffee. One anonymous donor bought everything I asked for, and shipped it to me. It was effortless.

Don't be shy about spreading the word that you need support. As soon as our work got underway, I went to family and friends, to show what we'd accomplished. I also talked about how much *more* I could do if I had the funding. "Look at this great program! I'm dying to expand it, but I can't without $10,000 from a major donor!" That's how Found Animals came to partner with us.

You'd be amazed how many people want to support an effort once they see that it's succeeding. You can use early successes to persuade more companies to donate a product you need, like dog food. Again, always keep track of statistics and results – we handed out this much food, we spayed and neutered this many animals in these three zip codes.

A few more points about money

Many animal welfare groups decide at some point to file papers to become a 501c3 organization, aka a nonprofit. The benefits are real: An exemption from federal and/or state corporate income taxes, the ability to apply for grants available only to IRS-recognized groups, and of course, the ability accept donations that are tax-deductible to donors. I'm going to argue that you shouldn't be in a rush to file those papers, which can cost a few thousand dollars. When you start, you don't know how long you'll be in business – you may not even know that you *should* stay in business, since after you begin doing research, you might find that it makes more sense to link up with other groups or even join an existing organization. One of the most essential requirements for doing this work well is being able to keep your ego in check.

You also could find an existing nonprofit to serve as your physical sponsor and "piggyback"; that is, make an arrangement in which donors contribute to the other group, with the money earmarked for you. In the early days of Downtown Dog Rescue, I met Sondra Davis, president of Friends for Animals, when she responded to a picture I'd posted online of dogs in a trash-filled parking lot. Sondra and I were and are opposites – her background was cat rescue, and she had very negative feelings about the people I was trying to help – but she was organized, financially stable, and did everything by the rules. I trusted her. So when she told me that if I raised my own money, I could run it through her 501c3, I didn't hesitate. I became the Vice President and a board member of her organization, and until June 2014, Downtown Dog Rescue was part of Friends for Animals. (In our original plan, I was going to take over for her when she retired, but instead I chose to go out on my own.)

If you consider using a physical sponsor for donations, you need to be very clear that you and your sponsor see eye-to-eye on money. You need to have budget meetings, and if you're applying for a grant, you need to be sure they understand that grant money is restricted, and will respect where it can and can't be used. If your partner seems to be too casual – "oh, what does it matter, a dog's a dog" – or worse, if he or she is someone who might be tempted to dip into your funds in an emergency, promising to pay you back later, that's not a someone to work with. Having a written agreement is a good idea. So are frequent meetings and communication. Because this relationship is so tricky and visions can diverge, I don't recommend doing this as long as I did. A better idea is no more than six months.

Another way to avoid the trouble of becoming a nonprofit is to see if your local shelter would write a grant proposal for something you want to do – they would administer the funds, and you'd do the actual work of running the program. Often, a shelter will be leery of asking for money to begin a new program because it will require them to hire additional staff. But if you're providing the staffing at no cost, it's value added for them.

One last piece of funding advice: Diversify. We are endlessly appreciative of Found Animals, but they're not our only donors – and they can't be. No matter how generous and supportive a key donor might be, you have to have others as well, as fallback. The furniture company I work for has some major customers, but we make sure they're not our *only* customers. If they decide not to buy from us in the future, it'll hurt, but it won't bankrupt us. An intervention program has to work the same way. You can't know what's going to happen. A donor may have financial problems, or there may come a time when you don't see eye to eye.

Finally, if you're considering doing any activity that involves a park, a store, or a crowd, you need to look into liability insurance in case someone gets injured. (We also have our volunteers provide an emergency contact sheet, and sign a waiver.) This may be a hard check to write, but it's an important one, and part of operating in a businesslike way. Our yearly premium is almost $4,000, which includes covering our kennel. Without the kennel, it might be a third that much.

Assess and reassess

Don't be afraid to tell people you trust the details of your plan, and when you do, listen to their feedback. The comments that matter most are those that are critical – both of what you want to do and of the people you want to serve. You'll learn a great deal about the negative assumptions others make about your target population, and part of your work will be teaching them the truth. You may also become aware of weaknesses in your program's structure. Take time to work out these problems. Keeping your plan fluid and adaptable is important, as long as what doesn't change are your ethics and commitment to serve people with pets well.

Finally, reassess your ability to come through. Jo Barker, a homeless single mom who I met around 2000 taught me a lot about the realities of being poor. Jo was often argumentative and difficult for anyone to get along with when she was mad – I always thought her anger masked depression – but she was smart.

"Poor people are always being told some new program will save them, then it turns out they live on the wrong block or zip code," she told me. "So don't come to my side of town, hold a press conference and act like a hot shot if you're not going to come through."

I've never forgotten those words. When you promise something then fail to deliver, it makes people mad and cynical. Promise less if less is what you can deliver. And once you've promised to do something, *do it*, whatever that takes.

***

**Starting a Shelter Intervention Program:
Key Points**

- **Pick a target community**
- **Get to know it and its people intimately**

- **Pick a problem that arouses your passion**

- **Assemble an intervention team**

- Make strategic alliances

- Consider how you'll handle money (and make sure your own finances are in order)

- Whatever you do, collect data

- Be aware of what you can address and what you can't

- Reassess the plan – and only make promises that you can keep

***

Chapter 3: Shelter Intervention -- The Daily Reality

It was just another day in South LA. Shelter staff sent a tearful dog owner to Amanda after she explained she couldn't afford to redeem her beloved 10-year-old dog, who'd been impounded. Why had the animal ended up in the shelter? Well, she was homeless, and a friend had generously offered her a place to shower, but said she couldn't bring her dog inside. She left the dog in her car, but because she wasn't familiar with the neighborhood, parked on a street marked no parking. She had outstanding tickets, so her car was towed –the tow truck driver brought the dog in. Now she owed over $300 to reclaim her car *and* the pet redemption fee. She had $50 to her name.

Barley's family also cried in the surrender line. They'd brought their young Shih Tzu to the shelter because they gotten notice that they'd be evicted from their Section 8 apartment if they didn't get rid of him. When they first found Barley on the street three years ago, they knew the landlord had a "no pets" policy. But they also knew that other renters in the complex had dogs, and figured no one cared about enforcing the rule. They were right – until the day a new management company took over. Anyone familiar with Section 8 knows how incredibly difficult it is to find housing. This family also had a young child who was happy in the local school; moving would utterly disrupt her life. They were devastated to surrender their dog, but what else could they do?

J.B., a tall, bearded white-haired man in his late 50s walked into the office to give his three beloved poodles, two six-year-olds and one that was 15. J.B. was a veteran who'd recently become homeless; he had found new housing that would accept animals, but couldn't move in for three weeks, and until then his best option was a bed at a VA shelter across town, which didn't allow dogs.

These five wanted and loved pets unnecessarily bound for the shelter (and possible euthanasia) illustrates the need for what we do. For the first woman, we paid the redemption fee. For Barley's family, Amanda spoke to the Section 8 apartment management company and negotiated permission for them to keep Barley if we paid a $300 pet deposit. (As a bonus, we made sure Barley was immediately neutered, vaccinated and microchipped at the ASPCA spay/neuter clinic next door. And after Barley's owners met a neighbor, a senior citizen, who'd also gotten an eviction notice because he had an aged cocker spaniel, we wrote a pet deposit check for him, too.) J.B.'s situation was more complex. He was slow to trust and his dogs needed vet care, so at the beginning, we paid for a night in a nearby motel, so he could stay close to them. Meanwhile, Amanda found a community partner and DDR volunteer who were willing to foster the dogs until J.B. got settled. (He also got a letter from his doctor stating he needs his pets for emotional support.) As often happens with Section 8 housing, getting J.B. into a new home has taken longer than expected; as I write, we're still helping him negotiate his situation.

There's no "typical" day in a shelter intervention project, except that every one brings surprises, tears, frustrations, and small triumphs. The specifics of what we see may be particular to our shelter and location, yet I believe any intervention program in an at-risk community will deal with similar challenges. To meet them requires creativity, fast thinking and patience. If you want to boil down our model to its essence, it would be something like "Get from problem to solution quickly and without drama, and in a way that empowers and involves everyone."

In general, we confront two basic situations: people's pets have been impounded by animal services and they can't afford to reclaim them, and owners have come into the shelter having made the difficult decision to surrender them. Animals get impounded for different reasons – they've been found running loose, they escaped the yard, got lost – or they've been taken, perhaps during a law enforcement action. A lot of judgment gets attached to people whose animals are confiscated or surrendered. I hear it all the time. "If people can't take proper care of an animal, they shouldn't have one at all. Pets are a luxury, not a right."

Let's look at that argument.

How can people "lose" their pets? Why do they have them at all if they can't care for them properly?

These days, many people are proud to announce that their dog is "a rescue." In neighborhoods like South L.A., you don't see much organized rescue, with its adoption fees, contracts and home checks. Informally, though, it's everywhere. Yes, sometimes people buy pets from a backyard breeder or a kid selling puppies in a parking lot. Mostly, though, pet ownership is the result of an unplanned good deed. If you spend time in a poor community, you'll see lots of animals living on the street, in back alleys or under abandoned houses. Those are the dogs and cats that people of the community often bring into their homes. People take in the cat left behind by a neighbor who moved, or the dog who was being abused. They adopt a puppy because "my cousin's dog had a litter and one was left and someone had to take her." They make a home for the stray "my son found in the schoolyard, covered with fleas." They do it because they feel sorry; because they're churchgoers and Jesus would say it was the right thing to do. "I can't afford this animal," they admit, "but it needs me, so how can I say no?"

People without money – some of the families we serve get by on less than $1,000 a month -- love animals as much as the affluent do, and most of them try to be responsible. They may succeed for months, even years, and then an emergency hits: someone's evicted, deported, dies, a home gets foreclosed, an apartment building is sold, the landlord changes his mind about pets. Everything falls apart.

I can't tell you how many times we've found pet owners standing in front of the shelter cages of their impounded animals crying. We see kids wailing. It costs about $157 to redeem an intact pet in Los Angeles, $67 for one that's neutered and microchipped. For a minimum wage worker, that's a day's pay. If the pet wasn't vaccinated, licensed or microchipped, all that has to be done (and paid for) before the pet can be redeemed, and an animal over four months old has to be sterilized. *And* the pet owner has to show ID that matches where he or she now lives.

Helping families pay redemption fees is a no-brainer. Because it's important that they be part of the process we always ask for their participation: what portion of the money owed they can afford to contribute. If the answer is $5.00, we'll take it. Then we cover the rest, also connecting people to the veterinarians and clinics with whom we have partnerships.

It's often more complicated to help them address the problem that landed their pet in the shelter in the first place. Maybe the family's fencing was inadequate and the dog got out. Maybe the animal was impounded because it was being kept tied up -- not because the owner meant to be cruel, but because that was the only way to keep it in the yard.

Our small crew of paid and volunteer workers fix fencing if that can be done, and build dogs runs if it can't. (Some landlords won't let tenants reinforce existing fences and even threaten them with the loss of their security deposit if they do.) If it looks as if the dog will be living outside, we buy and bring in a dog house. (Yes, I wish the dog would be allowed inside, too, but remember, we work with what is. Maybe next week that dog will be in the kitchen, and ultimately, on the couch.) We have a wonderful bilingual handyman who is a genius at repurposing items that have been donated or found discarded on the street. If we must, we purchase supplies from Home Depot, aiming for cost efficiency, and safety. Our leading question is: How can we make this work so that dog, the family and their neighbors are all happy and safe?

Sometimes pets end up in the shelter because their owners lack education – and I use that term loosely, to mean lacking life skills, not just a school diploma. Take this fairly common scenario:

Dad got a few parking or traffic tickets. There was no money to pay them, so he stuck them in a drawer and pretended they'd go away. Of course that didn't happen. Time passed, a judge issued a bench warrant, and eventually Dad got pulled over and arrested. The dog was in the car, so when Dad went to jail, the dog went to the shelter. Since Dad hadn't committed a real crime, he got out right away, but there was the dog, which his kids had had loved since it was a puppy, redeemable for cash he didn't have.

Was Dad partly at fault here? Sure. He ought to have paid those tickets before they became a crisis. But I doubt there's any one of us who hasn't done something similarly dumb -- got stuck with a penalty because we put off paying a bill, or procrastinated doing something important then pulled an all-nighter to try to meet the deadline. When you don't have financial resources, the consequences are bigger.

Shouldn't Dad have learned about responsibility a long time ago? Most of us live surrounded by friends who occupy the same educational and financial level we do; we learn how the world works by talking to those people. I live in the world of retail, design, and rescue. Many of the people I know are highly educated; I can get on the phone and within 15 minutes be connected to a specialist who can treat any animal problem you can name. People in poor neighborhoods live surrounded by neighbors who are unemployed, recently out of jail, possibly self-medicating through the use of drugs and alcohol. A high crime rate keeps everyone trapped. In some places, nobody even leaves home after dark.

A lot of the information that gets passed along is wrong. *Your dog has mange? Best to treat it at home; a vet will be expensive and assume it's your fault.* Professional role models are scarce -- friends can't teach how to create a resume or what to say in a job interview. Others living from paycheck to paycheck or on assistance can't teach budgeting or that it's prudent to put aside a little money each week to handle an unexpected expense like a traffic ticket. My old friend Jo Barker taught me how hard it is even for those who try to do everything right to escape poverty and "move up."

"Say I live in South LA and don't have a diploma, but there's a chance for me to go to school and learn a new trade," she said. "The problem is the program is it's

20 miles away in Van Nuys, and to get there, I'd have to take seven buses."

"Couldn't you move?" I asked.

"Except I have a subsidized apartment that I waited five years to get, and there's a ten year wait to for a new one."

"Can you buy a car and drive?"

"My assistance is $137 a month and food stamps. How can I afford a car? Even if someone gave me one, I couldn't pay for gas."

Sometimes the people we serve are dealing with situations so complicated that those of us with middle-class lives can't even begin to comprehend them.

Consider Cassandra, a middle-aged mother, whose five dogs and a cat were impounded by animal services. All had been living peacefully in a small bungalow until Cassandra made the mistake of allowing her son, recently out of prison, to move home. We never learned what illegal activity he'd been accused of committing, but it was was serious enough that the LA Police Department got a warrant for his arrest, as well as search warrant to enter Cassandra's home. While she was at work, they broke down her security door and front door, tore off her metal gate, tore drywall off the walls, took an air conditioning duct out of the ceiling and left her home wide open and exposed. Meanwhile the animals escaped to run into the street – including two senior dogs and a cat that had never been outside. Thankfully, the police officers saw the problem and called Animal Control, who picked them up and took them to the shelter for safety.

Neighborhood criminals, who realized that the dogs were gone, broke into Cassandra's car during the night.

We met her, because sympathetic neighbors drove her to the shelter three days in a row, where she cried and tried to figure out some way to get her pets back. She was faced with six separate impound fees, on top of whatever it would cost to fix her car and secure her home. I think a lot of people in her position would have given up.

The challenges of poverty are overwhelming and physical. Being poor not only increases the risk of obesity, but the likelihood of developing asthma and other lung diseases. According to the American Lung Association, low-income and minority Americans live in areas with worse air quality than the affluent. Some research suggests that the mental stress of being poor causes high blood pressure and cholesterol, as well as diabetes. Poverty imposes what I call a "tax" on the brain. A 2013 study done in Canada concluded that it used up so much mental energy it was equivalent to a 13-point drop in IQ.

Poverty increases stress which breeds instability which results in disorder that is multi-generational, multi-layered, and often so overwhelming that people can't think clearly enough to make good decisions at all. So they make poor choices – choices that negatively affect their own lives, and those of their pets.

Why help Dad and Cassandra? Because everyone needs help sometimes. Because it does no good to take their animals, which will suffer in the shelter. Because it does no good to tell them how badly they screwed up – they already know, and if we make them feel even worse, next time they won't bother to talk to us at all. Our job is to address the immediate problem, hopefully in a way that teaches something they can use in the future. After they meet us, they know they can make a call to ask for help. And as we do the intervention, we talk about the importance of not putting off fines, of the usefulness of microchipping, about the fact that having a spayed/neutered dog means lower licensing fees. We discuss how taking action -- fixing the fence so the dog won't get out -- can avert crisis. In some cases, part of what Amanda does it helping people understand how to talk calmly to those in power, such as animal control officer, or even police officers.

The shelter intervention problems helps animals and people, by giving them a sense of power and agency, because so little else in their life does.

A vital part of the intervention program's work is helping owners who have made the decision to relinquish their pets. What kind of person would do that? Surveys, including one done by the National Council on Pet Population Study and Policy whose researchers spent a year in 12 U.S. shelters, have pinpointed some of the major reasons people give:
- We can't afford to keep it.
- We can't cope with its bad behavior.
- We don't have time for it.

- The landlord changed his mind / We're moving, and the new place won't take pets.
- The animal is injured or sick.
- The animal is old.

Many of us in animal welfare have a hard time accepting these reasons, which we tend to call excuses. Giving up a pet seems so cold, such a betrayal. We talk critically about anyone who'd "dump" his or her pet, especially if it was old. "Watch, he'll walk out of here with a new puppy!"

"Why do *these people* get pets if they can't afford to train/treat/keep them?" we ask, then announce that "I'd rather live on the street than give up my dog."

Are some pet owners irresponsible, unfeeling assholes who get rid of the animals who love them, or breed puppies and dump the ones they can't sell? Sure.

But I haven't met many like that. I think it's easier for us in animal welfare to hate those who surrender pets than to try to understand them – and to address the complex range of problems that are likely to be behind the decision. It's easy to say 'I'd rather be homeless," when you know you'll never face that choice. Would you *really* be willing to sleep with your dog on a filthy, graffiti-covered street, where gangs control the area and physical violence is a constant possibility? It's also easy to believe hype and stereotype, especially when they confirm what we already believe. We all remember hearing about some guy who turned in his dog because "it got too big," but not about the broken-hearted woman who feels she has no choice because she's trapped in a domestic violence situation that makes her fear for the animal's safety, as well as for the safety of herself and her children.

I recently posted a story on Facebook about a family whose dog was hit by a car, was in terrible pain and desperately needed surgery. The family loved the dog, but came to the shelter to surrender it, because they couldn't afford to pay the mounting vet fees. Put yourself in their position for a moment. Your dog is suffering, and you have $20 in your wallet. No one you know can lend you a dime. You have no credit card, because you can't apply for one, because your boss pays you in cash, and you live in an illegally converted garage for which you also pay cash. What can you do? If you turn in the dog, at least someone will end its suffering.

Do we believe that this family doesn't love their dog as much as any of us? How can we even ask? And yet comments on my post included this one: "I'm sorry, those are all excuses...They could call around to vets and get pricing. It just boils my blood at how easily pets are given to the pound because people are plain lazy."

We rarely see a scenario in which surrendering a pet is done "easily." I'll never forget the mother who came to the shelter with her ten-year-old daughter one afternoon to give up their two little terrier mixes. She was beside herself. They'd moved into a new apartment, and because they saw lots of other families with pets, assumed keeping that theirs would be okay. But when the landlord realized they had dogs, he threatened to evict them. That would have ruined them financially, as they would lose their security deposit and everything they'd spent on the move. When the little girl, who was developmentally challenged, understood what was going on, and that she would leave the shelter without her dogs, she clutched them, crying so hysterically that her facial muscles were paralyzed. Amanda thought she was having a stroke and called paramedics. We offered the landlord a $500 pet deposit and I wrote one of the letters of my life, explaining the situation. We were able to have the dogs classified as service dogs (and of course we had them spayed and licensed). When we posted information on what had happened, a local Girl Scout troop and our supporters raised funds to help. Now the girl has her two best friends at home, and the family is doing well.

No one can tell me this was a case of "these people" not caring. Our own data shows us that 75 percent of those who learned about our program when they arrived at the shelter to surrender their pet accepted our help.

Let's look at the reality behind the common reasons for owner surrender in an economically depressed neighborhood – and how an intervention program can change the outcome.

"I can't afford this dog"

Our current arrangement with the South LA shelter places our counselor Amanda a small office next door to the main admitting area. People visiting the shelter learn she's there via a sign that says "How Can We Help You And Your Pet?" in both English and Spanish, or when a shelter staffer asks an owner if s/he might consider other options beside surrender. If the answer is yes, s/he is sent to Amanda's office.

"Are you here to give up your dog?" she will ask gently. "Can you tell me why? Is there something we can do to help you keep it?"

Each pet owner who agrees to our service fills out an intake form. We ask for basic information (assuring these pet owners that what they say will be kept confidential) but also race, income and a history of the pet in question, including the reason(s) for surrender. Some people accuse us of being "nosy." We explain that we need this information to qualify for the grants that fund us. (We will also keep a record of the intervention's outcome.)

After that, each conversation goes its own way. "You have to sit back and listen for as long as it takes," Amanda says. "Sometimes people just need someone to talk to – someone who will tell them it's okay to feel overwhelmed and upset. Someone they know is like them, speaks their language, treats them respectfully. Someone who doesn't react to them emotionally. People respond differently to difficult situations. Some people cry, some cuss, some lash out and blame you for not being able to fix things. You can't interrupt or bombard them with information. You really have only 10 minutes to change their minds, to let them see that a situation that seems hopeless has a possible other outcome."

Sometimes "I can't afford it" is surprisingly simple to resolve. As I said, many families in South LA are extremely poor. Some run out of money to buy food for themselves by the end of the month, so how can they possibly feed a pet? Thanks to donors who shop on our Amazon Wish List, we are able to provide pet food for anywhere from 30-50 families each month. Sometimes that, a bag of food – and being told that we are there to help for the new few months -- is all it takes.

Often, of course, it turns out that the immediate problem masks a deeper conflict. "I had a situation recently where a couple came in saying the dog was too expensive, but I could tell that it was the husband who wanted to get rid of it," says Amanda. "The woman had had the dog before they got married. I offered them three months of food. She said 'You'd really help me that way? I'm going to go home and think about it.' The next day, she called me and said she'd told her husband 'If you don't want to live with my dog, there's the door.' She just needed to know she support."

Not being able to afford a bag of food or required rabies shot may also be the tip of the financial iceberg -- conversation reveals that the pet owner is also moving in two weeks, to an apartment that requires a pet deposit, which she also doesn't have. Or a dog owner – a hostile, tattooed tough-looking young guy who reeks of marijuana -- can't afford to pay the "Notice to Comply" ticket that he got because his dog wasn't licensed or neutered but insists that it's "against his religion" to neuter the dog.

"I explained that he could fix the dog or pay a city-mandated breeder's fee," says Amanda. "He yelled "that's bullshit! You guys ain't right!' I said 'I don't make the rules. And was it against your religion to smoke a joint before you came into my office?' He calmed down, laughed and said 'You're crazy, but I like you. You're okay.' He went outside, made a phone call, and when he came back he agreed to the surgery. Two weeks later he came back and said 'You're crazy, but you're cool. Thank you.' This time, he smelled like cologne."

Obviously an intervention program can't eliminate everyone's problems or pay every bill. When our contribution can keep an animal out of the shelter, we give it. We also assess, listen, and try to formulate a plan *with* the pet owner. For instance, we always ask "How much can you contribute to this effort? Can you have a car wash or garage sale to raise some of the money?" It's important that people be invested in the process. We want them to have the experience of facing a problem that seems insurmountable, planning a strategy to tackle it, utilizing that strategy and succeeding. That memory will guide them the next time they face a challenge.

The animal is injured, sick, or old.

Very little enrages rescue advocates more than seeing old dogs limp into the shelter, those 15- and 16-year-olds that are blind, arthritic, tumor-ridden. What kind of person lets her best friend end its life in a cage alone? The answer maybe someone who doesn't know there are other options.

There are many pet owners who believe that surrender is the only way to end the suffering of an old or terminally ill animal. They've never heard about euthanasia, wouldn't know where to seek it out if they had, wouldn't be able to afford it in any case. Do you know how animals get put down in some of the countries that were the childhood homes of many of the families we help? Poison's one way. Another is to let a stronger animal finish it off. Do you know what inexpensive options are available here? I used hear stories about a vet tech, somewhere in LA, who for $50 in cash would take an animal through his back door late at night and use an overdose of anesthesia. You'd give him your pet, and never see it again.

I once met a homeless man, a Vietnam veteran, who told me that he'd lost a dog with cancer. I didn't get his meaning until he added, "You know, I have a gun," then started crying. The dog was in terrible pain, and he couldn't come up with the money to have it euthanized. And so he shot the dog, and he told me where he buried it. The memory still haunted him.

One of the most important services our intervention program provides – one of the most crucial that any intervention can provide – is offering humane euthanasia for terminal pets. Most of our pet owners have been profoundly grateful when Amanda asked "Would you like to stay with your dog to the end?" and explained that they could take their animal to a veterinary hospital to be euthanized painless and with dignity. This service allows animals to die peacefully, surrounded by those they love.

What if the pet isn't terminal but needs medical care that its owners say they can't afford? Again, let's not be dismissive or critical – which can be hard, if it's clear that the animal has been sick or hurt for a while. There are perhaps a tenth as many vets and animal care clinics in the South LA area as there are on LA's more affluent west side. And the price of care is no joke. The last time I took one of my dogs, a 15-year-old, to be treated for a minor ear infection, it cost $120.

"Some people actually think there's a vet at the shelter, which is part of why they consider surrender," says Amanda. "When they learn there isn't, they enter a vicious cycle: animal services now knows they have a sick animal, so they get a notice that they must seek medical care for it within 24 hours or be cited. Then they're facing a bill they can't afford. We offer a referral to a nearby low-cost veterinarian, who also offers payment plans. Often I'll look at the animal to get an idea what's wrong – I've been in rescue long enough that I can spot lots of standard problems – and estimate what treatment will cost. We talk about how much the owner can contribute, and how we might make up the difference – funds from us, credit, other foundations. I won't send anyone away just because our program can't cover it all.

"The other important lesson we teach is that a $3,000 quote for treatment isn't necessarily the bottom line. People don't realize they can get a second opinion or negotiate. They don't know that it's possible to agree to some but not all recommended treatment – to pay for an x-ray, for instance, but say no to the blood panel or other tests that the veterinarian wants to run 'just in case.'"

An aside: Through our clinics and partners, we *always* provide vouchers for free spay and neuter services to anyone who wants them. No zip code requirements, no breed requirements, no income test. No need to put your full name and address on a list.

We can't cope -- "this is a *bad dog.*"

People on all sides of town forget that the cute puppy that won their hearts won't know to pee outside or resist jumping on house guests without being taught -- and that teaching a pet good behavior takes time and work. Untrained, unruly pets are no fun for anyone; in fact, a prime cause for relinquishment is misbehavior: jumping, digging, lunging, fence-fighting with another animal, or suddenly showing aggression towards another dog in the house. The irony is that this is often an easy problem to address. We've solved fence-fighting issues just by putting up a divider, such as a sheet of metal, between two yards, and resolved destruction complaints by teaching owners about handling high-energy animals and those that easily get bored.

We also refer dog owners to our volunteer trainers. "You'd be amazed how many people don't know how to walk a dog properly, or which collar to use," says Amanda. In one instance involving two male dogs that had suddenly started fighting, after the owner met with Larry Hill of Puppy Imprinters Academy, he scheduled an appointment for both dogs to be neutered, then took a five-week course of training to help him better control and manage them. DDR also sponsors free dog training in a Compton park for dogs living in the Southeast community of the LA area. We keep things flexible and loose; you can drop in and out of the class as your schedule permits. Our only rule is that dogs must be spayed or neutered by the fifth class. Those who complete the class receive graduation certificates.

Does that sound hokey? Do you know how many times I've seen people cry when the certificates were given out? One woman, around 60, broke down. She said "I never finished high school. I never got a diploma or a certificate in anything. I'm so proud of myself and my dog!"

The landlord says no.

This is a real heartbreaker. Finding a rental that's affordable and pet friendly is getting harder and harder. A lot of landlords won't accept large dogs, or certain breeds. In LA, and in other big cities, not only are pet deposits going up, some landlords are charging extra "rent" for animals, as much as $50 a month.

An intervention program can offer a variety of solutions to families who feel they must relinquish a pet to keep their homes. We begin by making people aware of their rights as tenants – Amanda has a printed guide that she hands out. We also make them conscious of their own responsibilities. When someone comes in angry, complaining about the landlord "who's always hated me," we try to have a conversation about how the situation developed.

The landlord hates you? Are there any reasons why? Do you pay your rent on time? No? How many times were you late this year? Let's think about how that affects the landlord's thinking about your dog.

If we reach out to the landlord to mediate, we try to do it in a personal way. I know myself from running a business why he or she may be reluctant to accept our family's animal. Maybe the fact that they can't afford the deposit suggests they're unstable. They'll stop paying rent, the dog will wreck the place, then get left behind when they move out. Maybe the dog has already done some damage, like scratching up a door. But what if we offer to pay the pet deposit? What if we replace the damaged door with a better one, get the dog into training, and promise to take custody ourselves if there are more problems? If the answer's still no, we've been able to have some dogs trained and classified as service animals.

If we're unable to resolve the problem, the next step may be re-homing the animal or helping the family find a pet-friendly rental. Occasionally we pay for short term boarding or provide a foster home for pets belonging to people who are in transition, keeping the animal safe until it can go back home. We've also paid for a short term motel stay for people, and for people *with* their pets.

***

Shelter Intervention Daily Reality: Key Points
How can intervention address the problems that cause people to lose their pets?

- **Redeem animals that have been impounded by paying redemption fees**
- **Help keep animals from getting out again through simple home improvements**
- **Help people plan ahead to avoid emergencies that can result in animal impound**

How can intervention change the mind of an owner who wants to surrender

- **Help cover costs of food, medical care, spay and neuter services**
- **Offer humane euthanasia**
- **Educate owners about medical care options**
- **Offer access to training**
- **Cover pet deposits and/or mediate with landlords who don't accept pets**

***

Chapter 4: Best Practices in Shelter Intervention

What makes an intervention program succeed is not just *what* it offers but *how*. This is what we've learned works.

Creatively tailor and target outreach:

In the community we serve, people aren't living on Facebook and Twitter, so to reach them requires a more old-school, grassroots approach. As we first moved into the area, we held a hip-hop block party as a large-scale spay/neuter event. We've followed up with programs with tongue-in-cheek names like "Pimp your Pit" (a day of free sterilization and vaccinations). We had artists painting murals, and passed out collars, leashes, dog food and other supplies. Everything was free. When we introduced our monthly spay/neuter clinic using a mobile clinic at East Rancho Dominguez Park in Compton, I needed to get the word out. I saw how people loved ice cream and that there were trucks stopping by the park every hour. So I spent $100 to buy out one of those trucks for the afternoon, then had the driver sit in the middle of the park with stacks of flyers about an upcoming clinic. I hired the local loudmouth to walk around shouting "Free ice cream!" Everyone – even the kids across the street at a birthday party -- walked over. They took flyers home, and they met me. Other times, I've booked a local taco man to give away tacos and sodas. Our events have featured free sterilizations, microchipping, flea treatment, dog collars and leashes, food, dog beds – with entertainment by local musicians and rappers. And always food for the people. I still go by what I learned on Skid Row, that there's something about offering free food that stops people from being mean. If you want to give me trouble, you have to remember that I've bought you ice cream and tacos.

Remove barriers to service

We don't require that people prove they live in a certain area or are "poor enough" to "deserve" our help. I'm often asked, "So how do you know the people you serve aren't taking advantage of your system? How do you know that the person you just helped won't take what you offer and dump the animal in the street?" The answer is I don't. But my experience has taught me that most people are honest. We in rescue are always saying "don't judge a dog by its breed; they're individuals." So are people.

Other ways we've removed barriers include not making arbitrary distinctions in choosing who to serve. If shelters are overrun with pit bulls or Chihuahuas – as is true in Los Angeles – it may sound great to have a spay and neuter day specifically for those breeds. But what happens if a pit bull owner shows up and also brings his poodle? Why would you turn it away, when the result would be poodle puppies?

We find it's helpful to promise confidentiality. Low income people, especially undocumented people, may be afraid to talk honestly about where they live and where their money comes from. Unless what they tell us suggests a person or animal is being harmed or put in danger, everything is between us.

Tailor solutions, so they're both effective and meaningful

It's not useful to offer a pet owner free goods or services if those things do nothing to address the problem she's presented. It may be a great accomplishment that you've successfully gotten a pet store to donate dozens of bags of dog food, leashes and collars, but you can't offer any of those things to someone whose pet is sick, with vet services financially out of reach. When we craft solutions, we find we need to think them through three or four steps out. If the dog is barking nonstop because it's kept tied up, we can't just advise "untie it." We need to think about *why* that rope is there. It may turn out that there's no fence in the yard, so if the dog is free, it will escape, end up in the shelter or get hit by a car.

Aim to build long-term relationships

As I've said, I believe that the work of a successful intervention program is to *inform* pet owners, not pressure, compel or bully anyone into anything. Convincing a stranger to change the way he or she has been doing something, is all about convincing that person to accept new information or a new belief. To do that effectively, we in animal welfare must examine how we speak and think. Far too often we don't have real conversations with those we want to reach; instead, we preach at them. Someone turning his pet into a shelter, for example, doesn't need to be told how many dogs are dying there.

73

We also like to debate. That just means everyone talks past each other, each person more interested in what she's saying than in listening to the other. It's something that I've observed animal activists do a lot, in particular in our discussions with breeders. I'm not saying we should agree with what they tell us, but to go on simply repeating our argument is annoying and alienates those we truly need to reach.

Bullying someone, especially someone in crisis, may seem to work in the short term – perhaps the dog owner doesn't turn in his pet, and goes back home – but there's no way to know that he won't be back later; meanwhile, we've lost the opportunity to make a lasting connection. It's those connections that produce long-term positive outcomes for animals and people.

I remember talking to two young men at one of our Watts clinics, guys who told me proudly that they were planning to breed their pits and create their own line of puppies to sell. I was going a mile a minute about how important it was for them to neuter their animals instead, and they weren't hearing a word I said. Finally, I stopped and listened to them. Here's what I learned: They loved their dogs, but they'd never been to the local shelter, and didn't realize how many pits ended up there. They didn't need to be yelled at, they needed information.

Recall that the free, drop-in/drop-out obedience classes that we offer in the park require animals to be spayed or neutered by the fifth class. We've had great success accomplishing two things at once with this rule. Many of the men who've come the class started with the idea that they didn't want to neuter their dogs. They'd heard a lot of misinformation that suggested their dogs would get fat or change in temperament. We were able to advise them what a neutered animal looks like, and of the real benefits of neutering and spaying: reduced risk of uterine infections and breast cancer for females; for males, fewer problems with roaming and fighting, and no testicular cancer. (At the shelter, Amanda keeps some very graphic photos on her cell phone for anyone who needs extra persuasion.) All of them agreed to have their dogs neutered. *They* made the decision. This is important, not just because their dogs won't help make puppies, but because they'll pass the correct information about sterilizing to their friends and children, introducing a new tradition into the community.

We emphasize building long-term relationships because we know that due to the ongoing challenges people face, we may resolve one problem only to confront another later. We let everyone who works with us know that we will always be there for them. They can always talk to us; they can always contact us if they need help.

Learn how to hear those who disagree, or are resistant

Don't write someone off just because he or she is angry or seems without emotion. You may not know at first how people feel inside. Think of the word that describes what people are doing when they come into the shelter with a pet: surrendering. They know they've failed. Their children are sad or furious with them. (On

Facebook, I see posts from people in their 50s who still talk with rage about "the day my mom gave my dog away!")

It's important to listen, even when the conversation has nothing to do with animals. Amanda and I have both found that it's useful to echo what men and women say to us, which lets people them they're being heard. "It does sound like everything has gone wrong." "Yes, I know you feel that everyone is against you." From there, we can move the conversation to another level: I'm not telling you what to do, but I must tell you what will happen if you do nothing. If you don't address this ticket, there will be penalties and fees that add to its cost. If you don't resolve the issue of your dog being kept tied up, you could be charged with cruelty. If you already have a criminal record, this will add to it; having more charges may affect other parts of your life, such as the ability to have custody of your child. Why not work with me to find a way to eliminate the problem now?

Avoid being judgmental

Quiet your inner voice. You know the one I'm talking about – the one that offers a running commentary of your own opinions when you're listening to someone. That voice keeps you from hearing what the speaker is actually saying.

Assume everyone is a potential ally and will be if you work hard enough at it. Try to find out where you have overlapping interests.

Act curious whether you are or not. The next time someone shares information with you, ask questions.

You'll engage, learn more, and just the act of questioning will help you remember what you heard.

Do your best to understand the world the other person is living in. I've talked a lot about the stresses of poverty. You can't forget that the people you'll see have far bigger worries than taking the dog out for a walk every night. As part of the above: Don't judge people on the basis of how they look or what they own. At one of our clinics in Compton, people came in driving some nice cars. We see owners visiting their pets in the shelter talking about what they can't afford, while carrying the latest iPhone and wearing $200 Uggs.

There's a good chance the young man driving the nice car has borrowed or leased it, or he lives with his mother, and this is the only thing he spends his money on. The young woman in Uggs may spend 80 percent of her disposable income on shoes and makeup. You and I might not choose to spend money that way if we were only making $15,000 a year. And if I had another 24 hours in my day, I've love to teach budgeting and finance alongside dog rescue. Yes, these young people might not be making the best choices. So help them, by listening more and lecturing less. Hopefully, they'll mature, and hopefully they'll hang around us long enough to learn. If they don't, at least their dogs won't have puppies. That's still a victory.

Nurture your strategic alliances

It's crucial to regularly interact with and stay connected to the shelter staff, and actively solicit their participation in what you're doing. They can be a valuable resource. Not long ago, it occurred to me that since part of what animal control does is go into the community and give citations, why not use these officers to let people know about the resources we offer? I took my idea to one who referred me to his captain. The South LA officers now pass out our cards.

Make good use of social media

I'm very active on Facebook (though not as good as I should be on Twitter) and blog regularly on Downtown Dog Rescue's own website. I talk about the clinics and community events we sponsor, and give detailed stories, with pictures, of the families we've helped. We have 2,600 Twitter followers and 13,000 Facebook fans, though I'm less concerned with numbers than reaching people who'll support our work, including donating on a more expensive than usual care or helping out with transport. Being able to show exactly what we're doing and how we're helping in ways both big and small lets donors we already have see that their money is working, and encourages them to give more.

Social media is also very helpful in educating the public about the intervention program. We're all inundated with sad stories of pets being abused and neglected, something that is actually more rare than we believe. What we don't hear about is the reality of poverty -- the struggle involved in raising a family on $11,000 a year; the heartbreak of not having the money to buy medical care for a loved cat or dog. Told accurately and honestly, the stories we offer on social media bring that reality to tens of thousands of people.

In turn, I learn a lot from the responses these stories provoke, especially those that are negative. I don't get into a dialogue or try to argue and change anyone's mind; these responses help me see specific misconceptions I need to address in the future. Facebook analytics also help me understand how people respond to stories about different topics, which is useful information for fundraising purposes. (In the appendix, I've included some examples of intervention-centered Facebook posts, and one blog post.)

Always record the data

I said this before, but let me repeat: Funders, other nonprofits and your supporters want to know that you've done what you say you have. When you make a claim, you'll be asked "How do you know this? Can you prove it?" This is where the intervention team "math nerd" comes in. You must be able to answer those questions: We have worked with this many families, of this ethnicity, this percentage of whom were single moms... If and when you apply for grants to fund your work, data enables you to tailor a grant aimed at working with specific populations.

A side point about data: You need it, and it's extremely important in analyzing whether or not a program is making an impact. But be aware that it doesn't always tell the whole story. Take this kind of situation, which isn't unusual. An owner comes in to surrender a shy, intact, untrained and not-well-socialized black pit bull, because she has a no-license citation she can't pay. We cover the ticket, help her get a license, and give her a spay/neuter voucher. She sterilizes the dog, goes to our free training class, and in the months after, checks in regularly with our counselor. Then disaster strikes: she loses her job, then her apartment, and has to move in with her sister, who hates dogs. She couch surfs after the sister kicks her out; then, because she's still not working and can't make car payments, her car gets repossessed. Now she's careless, homeless, and her best chance to get back on her feet is to live in a shelter that doesn't allow animals. Surrendering the dog has become her only option.

The dog that we worked so hard to keep out of the shelter may enter it anyway. Does that represent a failure for our program? Statistically, yes. Realistically, not at all.

Imagine if our intervention team hadn't connected to that dog and owner earlier. A shy, black, untrained adult pit in a crowded shelter probably would have been euthanized in a week. Now, we know the dog, and feel like its owner is family. We'll actively network it and find a rescue to take it. When the rescue finds an adopter, the original owner will be told that her dog has a family again. To me, that's no failure.

Deliver!

I also said this earlier, but it's important enough to say again: If you are working in poor or underserved communities, you are working with people who've been promised a lot and seen those promises broken. Funding disappears. Volunteers burn out. The charter school that was supposed to change everything for local children suddenly closes its doors. When you offer help, people will seem suspicious, even ungrateful. Their experience tells them you won't come through. Defy those expectations. Never promise what you can't deliver, and always deliver what you say you will.

***

Shelter Intervention Best Practices: Key Points

- **Craft outreach tailored to the target audience**
- **Provide service that's easy to access and doesn't require proof of need**
- **Offer solutions that specifically address the problem at hand**
- **Build long-term relationships in the community**
- **Nurture allies, and listen to those who disagree**
- **Use social media to get the word out**
- **Record the data**
- **Always come through for the pet owners you offer to help**

***

Chapter 5: The Challenges of Intervention

As you begin an intervention program, be ready for a rollercoaster of intellectual and emotional challenge. The pace is relentless; the need never stops. There are hard choices to make every day – often, many times in a single day. You'll face

--the challenge of rationing a limited budget for medical care

We could pay for veterinary care all day long, and sometimes it kills me that we can't. Our budget is $300 per case, which honestly doesn't buy much, and the cap is always being pushed. Two dogs get into a fight – which happens even in the best of homes – and both end up bloody. The wounds need to be cleaned and sutured, the bill will be $1,000 and the owner has $100 in his pocket. That's when he brings the dogs to the shelter. What do we do? Allow two pets who have a home be surrendered or pay more than we've allotted for care?

Every day Amanda and I have to juggle and balance priorities. We spent $10 on this one, so we can spend a little more on the next... Then a teenager shows up in a panic, cradling a bleeding two-month-old puppy that just got attacked on a walk. Everyone's crying, and the next thing we know we've spent $2,500. Do that too much and you burn out your funders.

--The challenge of setting limits on what you do for people

While a shelter intervention program can do many things, it can't fix every problem and help every person who walks through the door. Trying to do too much can cause those running the program to burn out and even grow angry and resentful. It's also worth remembering that as difficult as it is to witness a pet owner fail, failing is one way people learn.

Setting boundaries for yourself and for your program is crucial. Solvency requires financial boundaries. It's a good practice to delegate financial oversight to at least one trustworthy and clear-headed person who'll make sure you're staying on track. You should have an overall program budget and a per-case budget, and a person or committee that the counselor can call or text if going over-budget on a case seems appropriate.

Mental boundaries are important as well. No one is good at handling all problems. If there are certain types of cases or phone calls that really get to you, speak up and make sure there is someone else in the group who can give you a break.

Setting practical boundaries could include deciding you'll take no text messages after 4:00 PM and no calls after 6:00, or that there will be certain days or times you won't be available discuss the program or its problems at all. **Do not feel guilty about taking some "me" or reflection time. You need and deserve it.**

Finally, a vital boundary is demanding respect. That means pet owners are not permitted to yell or curse at you. You do not allow them to project their problems and bad choices onto you, or let yourself be haunted by accusations like "So you're telling me you'll just let my dog die?" if you say you can't help. A respectful program atmosphere also means avoiding gossip, and making sure it does not occur in the office.

--The challenge of keeping yourself and your staff safe

When you run an intervention program, you will inevitably face people who are emotional, angry, or unstable. Keeping yourself, your volunteers and your staff safe is of the utmost importance. One rule I can I suggest is not getting involved in family issues or fights over pet ownership, which come up a lot in the program. Someone has a dog, is sent to jail, someone else cares for the dog while he's gone, then he comes home and wants his dog back... To me, the point is to help whoever has the dog to care for it now. We don't think about next year or who "deserves" to keep the animal. It's not your place, and potentially dangerous, to step in in that way.

In general, trust your intuition. You need to allow people who are angry to vent. Sometimes that's all they need -- their neighbors and friends are tired of hearing them talk about the dog problem, but you're a new person, so they're talking to you. If you sense that things are getting too tense, you can try to de-escalate by calmly making a plan, showing the person how that plan will operate, and taking the first step: "I'll send you home with this bag of dog food." You can also make the boundaries that I just discussed explicit: illustrating to the angry person exactly what you can and can't do.

Remember that you can't make everyone happy and there are times you will have to say, "I'm sorry, I can't help you."

Don't get pulled into a verbal battle with an angry person. Don't try to "win" an argument. If you start to feel physically threatened, if someone is yelling and getting too close, walk towards a shelter staff member or a volunteer, someone who can call the police if necessary. Sometimes you may have to do that. One pet owner Amanda worked with got furious at being told we couldn't help. She reached across the counter and tried to grab Amanda. A shelter staff member called the police, and Amanda now has a restraining order against the woman, who is not allowed to come back into the shelter. Thankfully, situations that extreme are rare.

--The challenge of withstanding pressure from others (including your rescue allies) to do things their way

There will be times the intervention goal of keeping a dog in its first home will seem less appealing than the option of sending it elsewhere. Friends will ask why you are jumping through hoops to keep a dog with a struggling family when there are more stable and affluent adopters out there. You may wonder yourself, when a dog is six months old, super-cute and you know wonderful people looking for that exact breed.

It's your responsibility to stay true to your mission. That means being honest about the situation, and telling the family that "If you surrender your dog, it's highly like she will get adopted. In fact, I know a rescue that's interested and I can call right now."

But if the answer's no -- "I don't want to surrender, I really love her" – then you must help the owner keep her dog.

--The challenge of accepting uncertainty

There's no way to know what happens to the animals you keep out of the shelter – or even whether you've kept them out forever. You don't know, you can't know, what will happen a month or year down the road.

That uncertainty doesn't mean you haven't succeeded on some level. Because you stepped in, the person you helped will have learned something new about animals and him or herself. If this pet gets surrendered eventually, maybe the next time the owner gets an animal, he or she will do better. Maybe the new information you gave will spread to his or her circle of friends. That's outreach and long-term improvement.

--The challenge of sometimes giving up on a case.

Not every situation in the shelter intervention office has a happy ending. There are times when people seem unwilling or unable to come through, no matter how hard you try. You can offer a medical voucher, but someone has to keep the appointment. You can provide access to training, but you can't make that person go. There are times when personal problems – poverty, family dysfunction, mental illness, substance abuse -- are too great. You have to stop asking for something a pet owner can't give, and accept that he or she can't change. In shelter intervention, you must accept that your work is to help, not to fix. If you don't, you risk hopelessness, anger, burnout.

Sometimes a pet surrender is inevitable. In the end, the decision is the pet owner's, not yours. Blame isn't productive. If possible, you want to keep working with these people, both to lessen the impact of what happen, and to make them better pet owners if they get past this crisis and decide to try again. When you keep people on your side, you're also able to get as much information as possible about the animal being surrendered, so both shelter staff and a rescue group will know its personality and history.

I'm human -- there have been times when a situation had me crying in my car, or thinking 'Maybe I shouldn't do this any more.'

But those moments don't last. Working to change outcomes for people and pets is the most gratifying and exciting thing I've ever done. I wake up every morning thinking 'Wow, I wonder what's going to happen today.'

***

Challenges of Shelter Intervention: Key Points
The need to
- **Not lose control of the budget**
- **Set emotional limits**
- **Accept uncertainty**
- **Know when to give up**

***

Chapter 6: Moving forward

In October of 2013, the ASPCA took note of our intervention program and asked us to explain what we did and how a national organization could expand the model. Today, the ASPCA runs its own intervention programs at the Downey and Baldwin Park Animal Care Centers (which are part of the Los Angeles County shelter system). We helped them find two of their three counselors, and I'm proud to say that Miguel and Bernice were both Downtown Dog Rescue volunteers first. And DDR remains involved; we assist in building dog runs, repairing fences and delivering dog houses. We work together collaboratively and well.

In addition, DDR worked with the ASPCA to conduct a research study on what families surrender their pets, what type of pets, and why they feel surrender is necessary. We'll always be grateful to this organization for helping us formulate a questionnaire that every pet owner now fills out when they accept our offer of services. This groundbreaking study is being used to dispel the myth that people who surrender are "dumping their pets." Instead, it proves what we already knew: that for people with pets who live in poverty, poverty is the main problem, and the assistance they need is practical and financial. People love their pets and consider them part of the family no matter what their income level.

I have a lot of dreams for the future. I'd love our South LA Program to receive a grant big enough to provide our full-time counselor a better wage and health insurance, and to hire handymen and dog trainers full time.

More globally, I envision creativity transforming animal care, especially for the poor. Imagine if cheap pet vaccinations, general care and spay/neuter vouchers were available from a tricked-out van or hip-hop food truck that would tweet its upcoming locations and announce its presence with great music.

Imagine cities full of the kind of mobile vet clinics run by the Sam Simon Foundation here in LA. These clinics do more serious vet work -- hematoma surgeries, even leg amputations for free. There's no lecture when you show up, just care for your animal.

Imagine vets in the local mall, between the Panda Express and Starbucks, and pet wellness clinics on the corner, right next to the children's dentist and $29.99 x-ray. Imagine that those clinics were high volume enough to make low prices possible.

We could make pet licensing easy, cheap and desirable by offering incentives: free food on licensing days; a promise that whenever Animal Services picked up a licensed dog, it would be held for a longer period of time, and redemption fees would be reduced or eliminated. Look at what's been done in Calgary, Canada – you can get your pet license in person, but you can also apply online 24 hours a day. When you do, you get a rewards card that gives you discounts at over 60 merchants. If your cat or dog is impounded, it's held an extra week before being put up for adoption, and impound fees don't kick in until the second day. That city now has the highest rate of pets returned to owners and the lowest euthanization rate in North America.

Finally, I envision a different kind of animal shelter –a place where pet owners can come for help, a community resource, a place where people in difficult situations can board their animals and keep them safe for a week or two. A *shelter* in the truest sense of the word, and one that brings in the enormous number of people who love animals but aren't currently involved in the animal welfare movement -- homeless people, poor people, recent immigrants. They will join us if we just reach out.

A shelter intervention program is a step in that direction. It's a movement towards changing our animal sheltering paradigm from "rescue" to "prevention." To both people and pets, it offers hope.

Appendix

Form that we give to vet to price out medical :

Pet Cat (no feral cats) for cats 4 months +
Spay/neuter Bundle Surgery + vaccines $

Pet Dog - no rescue dogs
Spay/neuter Bundle Surgery + vaccines $

Humane Euthanasia Small $ Large $
cats, rabbits and dogs
Vaccine package for cats $
Vaccine package for dogs $

LEVEL 1
Ear Infection $
Minor Skin Issues $
Simple Eye Issues $
Fecal + De-worming $
Sedation $

LEVEL 2

2 view radiographs (xrays) $

Mange Treatment $

Urinary Tract Infection $

Medical Grooming (severely matted pet) $

Full Blood work $

Feline URI Treatment $

Tooth abscess Treatment $

Minor wound care (may include suturing) $

LEVEL 3

Minor Mass Removal $

Basic Hernia Repair $

Outpatient Prvo Treatment $

Hematoma Repair $

LEVEL 4

Basic Dental $

Major Skin Issues (multiple visits to treat) $

LEVEL 5

Major wound repair (may require hospitalization)$

Hernia Repair $

Prolapse Repair $

Urinary catheter unblocking $

Major mass removal $

LEVEL 6

Pyometra $

Amputation $

Intestinal blockage

An example of how we track cases on a daily basis using

a Google-Doc

Date	1/1/2014	1/2/2014	1/3/2014	1/4/2014	1/5/2014
	Closed				
Pets intercepted	0	5	7	24	6
Dogs		5	7	22	5
Cats		0	0	2	1
Rabbit		0	0	0	0
Service Inquiry					
Mange		0	0	0	0
Euthanize		0	0	0	0
Too Expensive		0	0	1	0

Behavioral		1	0	2	0
Pet not allowed in housing		0	0		0
Pet needs to rescued/ rehomed		0	1	1	1
Total Excluding S/N	0	1	1	4	1
Spay/Neuter		4	6	20	5

Facebook Posts

Today at the South LA Shelter, a dog owner arrived by taxi with her senior dog who was clearly dying. According to Amanda, his face was swollen like a balloon, he could no longer hold up his head, he could not eat or drink. He had been diagnosed with throat cancer last week by The Sam Simon Foundation's Mobile Veterinary Clinic and was not a candidate for surgery. The tumors must have burst and she used her last $40 to take the taxi. Amanda couldn't let her surrender her dog to the shelter. She loaded up the terminally ill dog and his owner and drove them to Alondra Animal Hospital. Between sobbing tears, she explained that

94

she rescued him many years ago from an abusive neighbor that used to fight him. According to her, he had saved her life when she was very ill. When it was time and he made his transition, she screamed and cried in grief. Without the shelter intervention program, private humane euthanasia would not have been an option. Every pet and every person has a unique story that most of us can relate to if we listen. Everyone needs help sometimes.

Here is another post: Amanda's favorite SLA Shelter Intervention story of the day. This family had a sudden tragic death in their family and had to travel out of state for a month. With no friends or family to watch over their dog while they were gone, boarding him somewhere was also out of the question financially, surrendering him to the shelter was their only option. One month later, they came to the shelter to look for him and HERE HE WAS, still at the shelter, waiting to go home. They had $20 to pay the redemption fees, DDR paid the balance and another big dog went home! Many of you reading might think if that was me, I would find a way but often families can't even pay for a funeral for a family member, resorting to standing on a street corner with a donation jar and a sign. This is not just happening in Los Angeles, this is happening all over the United States. Some people can't afford to pay for basic needs, no way they can cover boarding a dog at a rate of $20 to $30+ per day for 30 days or more.

A story of hope from the South LA Shelter Intervention Program

Last week, a woman named Eusebia brought her dog Chucho to our South LA Shelter Intervention office, having lost all hope. Weeping, she could barely tell our counselor Amanda her story. How she got to this point. She and her children loved Chucho, but their landlord received a cancellation of the property insurance because Chucho was labeled a German Shepherd. She was given 72 hours to move or get rid of him. As a single mom out of work, barely covering rent and food, she was in no position to move. To make matters more complicated, she was battling a deep depression, suffering PTSD as a survivor of domestic violence. Like many families we meet, Chucho was their "rock". Sadly they all came to the shelter to say goodbye. The family had been up all night crying, thinking that they would never see their beloved pet ever again. Can you imagine how that might feel? Amanda read the letter from the insurance company. She took action by calling the landlord and then the insurance agent to get more information. What she discovered was that by getting Chucho to be categorized as a shepherd mix, combined with the fact that he was already neutered and licensed, he qualified to become a service dog for Eusebia, based on some personal medical information that she shared with Amanda.

But we had to overcome one more obstacle: The landlord wanted a letter, and the medical doctor was referring Eusebia to a specialist which would be a   month-long wait. She didn't have that much time, so we sent her to a doctor we work with and in less than two days, her case was completed. Not only did Chucho get to stay with his family, he was now able to go almost everywhere with them. The smiles on this families' faces was all Amanda needed to see. There are so many families with pets out there that need an advocate, that need help to get through a tough time. The Shelter Intervention Programs are now at the Los Angeles Animal Services' South LA Shelter, East Valley Shelter, and North Central Shelter, as well as several County Animal Care and Control shelter such as Carson, Baldwin Park, and Downey.

The Shelter Intervention Program is unique in that it creates customized solutions for families and their pets. Although it is a replicable program, we do not offer one-size-fits-all, cookie-cutter responses. We meet each family where they are, and problem solve to keep a pet in a happy home however we can. Rarely are two cases the same, and yet this is perhaps what makes it so exciting. It's a program that provides on the ground, real answers to questions that can make a difference between life and death. Just as Chucho who is still alive today, still prancing around his home, and still very much adored. It was our pleasure and honor to have helped Eusebia and her family. We look forward to the day where this model is carried out in more shelters, and in more cities.

561 clients were served from July, 2014 to January 30, 2015. The great majority of clients, 94%, sought services for dogs. About a third had pets at immediate risk of relinquishment, with the intention of leaving their pet at the shelter. About a third had pets at high risk of relinquishment, with the need for spay/neuter services and about a third was previous clients returning for more services. See table 1.

Table 1: Breakdown of reasons clients access DDR.

Initial reason for coming to the shelter		
Leave pet at shelter	191	36%
Spay/neuter voucher	159	30%
Continue previous work with DDR	185	35%
total	535	

Client Characteristics

Clients are predominately Hispanic females between the ages of 20 and 60. The primary languages were Spanish and English. More than half were single and had never been married. Only 40% were unemployed and only 38% had less than a high school diploma. 80% made less than $25,000 per year, but only about half were on public assistance.

Table 2: Client characteristics

Hispanic/Latino			
Yes	405	77%	
No	118	23%	
total	523		
Client's sex			
female	355	63%	
male	203	36%	
total	561		
primary language			
Chinese	1	.2%	
English	187	44%	
English/Spanish	12	3%	
Spanish	237	56%	
total	426		
Client age			
18-19 years	20	4%	
20-29 years	116	21%	
30-39 years	119	22%	
40-49 years	125	23%	
50-59 years	106	20%	
60-79 years	54	10%	
80 years or more	3	.6%	
total	543		
marital status			
Divorced/Widowed/Legally Separated	64	12%	
Married/Domestic	193	36%	

Partnership		
Single, never married	287	53%
total	544	
employment status		
full time	81	23%
part time	102	29%
Student/Retired	35	10%
Un-employed	139	39%
total	357	
education		
8th grade or less	66	13%
9-12th grade, no diploma	136	25%
Associates degree	18	3%
Bachelors degree	17	3%
High school diploma/GED	162	30%
Post Graduate work	6	1%
Some college, no degree	128	24%
total	536	
income		
<10K	120	29%
10-14,999	77	18%
15-19,999	85	20%
20-24,999	54	13%
25-29,999	39	9%
30-34,999	21	5%
35-39,999	8	2%
40-44,999	7	2%

45-49,999	1	.2%
50-54,999	2	.5%
60+	4	1%
Total	418	
Receiving public assistance		
Yes	264	49%
No	271	51%
total	535	

Interestingly, 99% of clients were the pets' primary caregiver and 80% had had the pet for at least 6 months. 519 people reported having adequate transportation to care for the pet.

Table 3:

Primary caregiver		
Yes	537	99%
No	8	1%
Total	545	
How long have you had this pet?		
Less than a month	18	3%
1-6 months	91	17%
6 months-1 year	101	19%
1-10 years	272	51%
More than 10 years	51	10%
total	533	
Access to		

transportation		
yes	519	

When asked if anything had changed in their household that led to the visit to the shelter, clients most frequently reported an inability to pay for the care of the pet.

Table 4: What had changed in the clients' lives. Note: clients could select more than one.

Moving	18
Landlord issues	67
Family illness/death	10
Behavior issues	20
Lack of time	14
Inability to pay for care of pet	480
New baby/children	4

Description of client's' home

Each household had an average number of 2.4 adults and 1.2 children living in the home.
Most clients, 81%, rent their home. See table 5 for a breakdown of home type.

Table 5: Breakdown of home type.

Apartment/condo	125	27%

Duplex/attached house	64	14%
Mobile home/trailer	7	2%
Single family home	268	58%
total	464	

Pets' characteristics

The average condition of the pets was 4.8 (normal is 5) with a range from 1-8.

Table 6: Pet characteristics.

Adult dog size		
Small	243	48%
Medium	87	17%
Large	174	34%
X-large	7	1%
total		
Pets' sex		
female	205	37%
altered female	66	12%
male	203	37%
altered male	80	14%
total	551	
Pets' age		
Less than 3 months	23	4%
3-12 months	98	18%
1-5 years	269	49%
6-10 years	109	20%
11 to less than 15 years	37	7%

15 or more years	13	2%
Don't know	2	.4%
Total	551	
Where was the pet living?		
Indoors only	223	41%
Outdoors only	162	30%
Indoor/outdoor	163	30%

Tracking the services delivered by DDR

Table 7: The frequency of services listed in the services tracking form.

Services	Frequency
Spay neuter referrals	165
Medical services	128
Microchip	45
Vaccines	39
Rescue	38
Redemption fees	30
Humane euthanasia	19
Fence install or repair	17
Financial assistance for housing requirements	10
Dog behavior training	6
Licensing fee	5
Provided:	

104

	Outdoor shelters	5
	Food	7
	Litter supplies	1
	Toys or enrichment	0

Mapping the locations of clients

The Downtown Dog Rescue maps include data for dogs and cats assisted by DDR between 7/2/14 and 1/9/15. There are 2 maps of just dogs (428 in the dataset) at two different scales (one is a zoomed in version of the other) and 2 maps with dogs and cats combined (428 dogs + 22 cats = 450 pets) at two scales (one zoomed in). The red/orange/yellow coloring indicates areas where greater numbers of pets came from, i.e. "hot spots".

"Do the best you can until you know better. Then when you know better, do better."

- Maya Angelou

Made in the USA
San Bernardino, CA
24 November 2015